Garfield rounds out

BY: JIM DAVIS

BALLANTINE BOOKS · NEW YORK

 Published in the United States by Ballantine Books, a division of Random House, Inc., New York, and simultaneously in Canada by Random House of Canada Limited, Toronto.

Library of Congress Catalog Card Number: 87-91860

ISBN: 0-345-35388-9

Manufactured in the United States of America

First Edition: October 1988

10 9 8 7 6 5 4 3 2

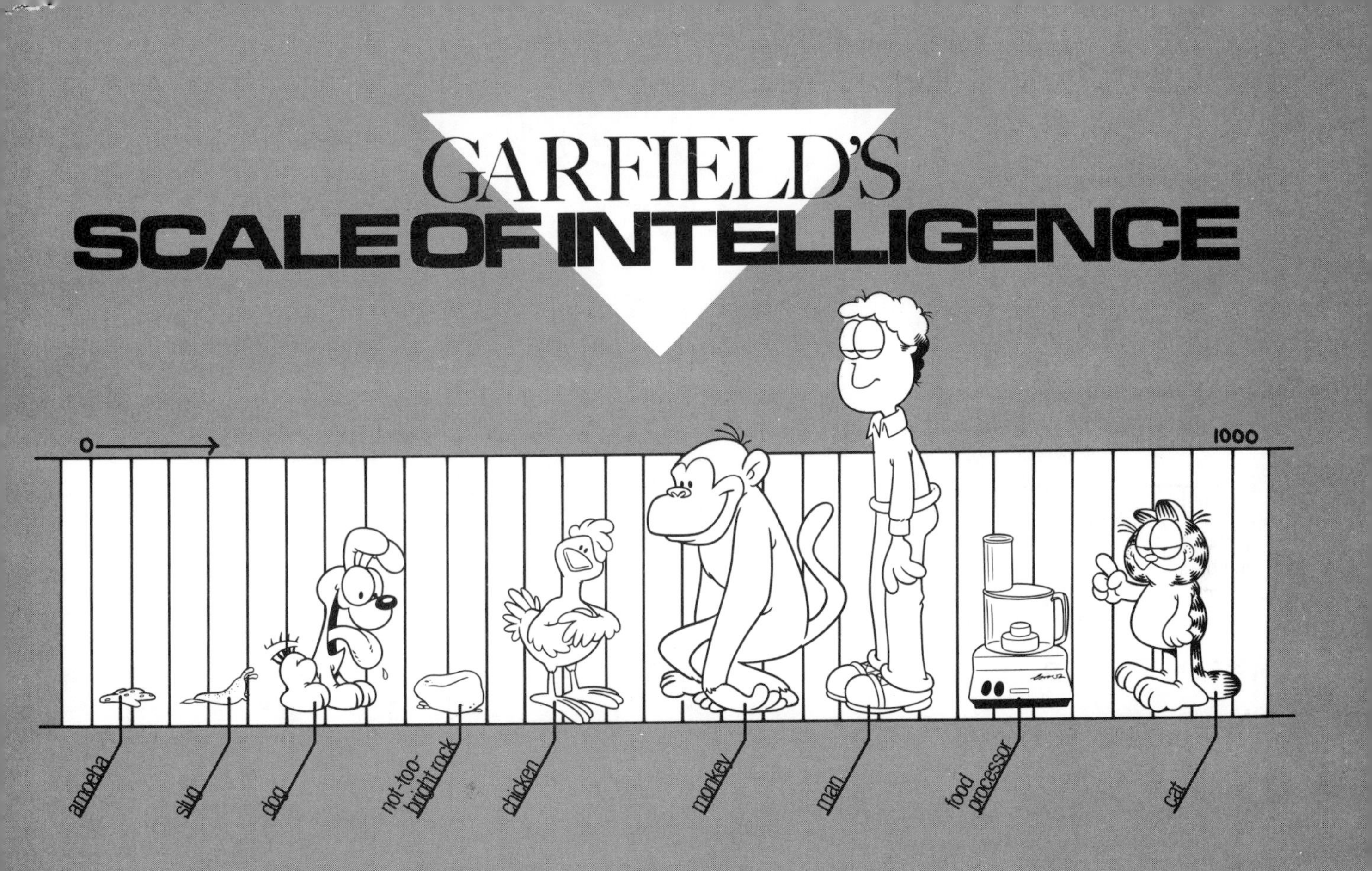
GARFIELD'S
SCALE OF INTELLIGENCE
0
1000
amoeba
slug
dog
not-too-bright rock
chicken
monkey
man
food processor
cat

BOY, I WISH I HAD A FIFTY POUND PAN OF LASAGNA
KRONG!!!
NOW WOULDN'T YOU THINK I'D KNOW BETTER THAN TO MAKE A WISH LIKE THAT ON A MONDAY
JIM DAVIS 5-18
© 1987 United Feature Syndicate, Inc.
THERE ARE MANY WAYS TO MAKE A DIET MORE APPEALING
SOME SAY IT HELPS TO DRESS YOUR FOOD UP
I SAY IT STILL LOOKS LIKE CELERY
JIM DAVIS 5-19
© 1987 United Feature Syndicate, Inc.

I HATE DIETS
THEY'RE MORALLY WRONG
A STOMACH IS A TERRIBLE THING TO WASTE
JIM DAVIS 5-20
© 1987 United Feature Syndicate, Inc.
OH, GARFIELD!
YOU'VE DONE SO WELL ON YOUR DIET I'M GIVING YOU A TREAT
OH MY GOSH! I'VE FORGOTTEN HOW TO EAT!
JIM DAVIS 5-21
© 1987 United Feature Syndicate, Inc.

LET ME PUT IT THIS WAY... HAVE YOU EVER CONSIDERED A CAREER AS A RIVER BARGE?
© 1987 United Feature Syndicate, Inc.
YOUR MOTHER WAS A BLENDER
THAT HURT
JIM DAVIS
5-22
COME ON, TAKE A CHANCE, WEIGH YOURSELF! I'LL BE KIND! TRUST ME!
© 1987 United Feature Syndicate, Inc.
BOY! ARE YOU FAT!
NOT TO MENTION GULLIBLE, TOO
JIM DAVIS
5-23

GOOD EVENING, LORI, MY DEAR. OUR DINNER AWAITS
© 1987 United Feature Syndicate, Inc.
YOUR STEAK, MADAM
PANT PANT PANT
ODIE! GET OUT OF HERE!
RRRRR
GIMME THAT!
LET GO! LET GO! LET GO!
PLOP!
5-24
AYIIIIEEEEE!!!
WHAT'S WITH HER?
PET HATER
JIM DAVIS

GUESS WHAT I GOT AT A GARAGE SALE TODAY, GARFIELD?
YOU GOT MY ATTENTION
TAH-DAH!
ISN'T IT GREAT?
THAT DIET MUST'VE BEEN MURDER, HUH, FELLA?
JIM DAVIS
© 1987 United Feature Syndicate, Inc.
5-25
I CAN'T BELIEVE JON ACTUALLY BOUGHT THAT THING. WHAT GOOD IS IT?
MAW! COME QUICK! THE COW'S SICK!
5-26
© 1987 United Feature Syndicate, Inc.
JIM DAVIS

HEY, MOM, GUESS WHAT I GOT AT A GARAGE SALE?
JIM DAVIS
I BOUGHT ONE OF THOSE COW SKULLS LIKE YOU SEE IN THE OLD WESTERNS
BEHIND YOU, JON!
HANG ON, MOM, I THINK I'M ABOUT TO SCREAM OR SOMETHING
5-27
© 1987 United Feature Syndicate, Inc.
GARFIELD, DID YOU KNOW EVERYTHING EVOLVES FROM A LOWER LIFE FORM?
I DIDN'T KNOW THAT!
5-28
JIM DAVIS
WHY, OF COURSE! IT ALL MAKES SENSE NOW!
ROCKS EVOLVED FROM DOGS!
© 1987 United Feature Syndicate, Inc.

GARFIELD! WHAT ARE YOU DOING?!
I'M UNRAVELING YOUR DENTAL FLOSS
I HATE THAT!
OH, VERY WELL. TOMORROW WE'LL DO SOMETHING YOU LIKE
© 1987 United Feature Syndicate, Inc.
HERE YOU GO, GARFIELD!
CRUNCH!
IT DOESN'T HAVE MUCH OF A SENSE OF HUMOR, DOES IT?
JIM DAVIS
5-30
© 1987 United Feature Syndicate, Inc.

© 1987 United Feature Syndicate, Inc.

JIM DAVIS 5-31

Z
ZZZ-ZZF-ZZZ-ZZ
MUST BE MONDAY
ZZZ-ZZF-ZZZ-ZZF-ZZZ-
6-1
© 1987 United Feature Syndicate, Inc.
JIM DAVIS
YOU KNOW, GARFIELD...
GARFIELD
I WOULDN'T SAY YOU'RE FAT, BUT...
GARFIELD
THEN DON'T
GARFIELD
6-2
© 1987 United Feature Syndicate, Inc.
JIM DAVIS

I BOUGHT YOU A SURPRISE TODAY, GARFIELD!
JIM DAVIS
IT'S A SWEATER MADE ESPECIALLY FOR YOU!
WIDE LOAD
© 1987 United Feature Syndicate, Inc.
LOAD
6-3
YAWN
I THINK THE OLD BLANKET IS DUE FOR A WASH
© 1987 United Feature Syndicate, Inc.
JIM DAVIS
6-4

WE CATS LOVE TO ROAM AROUND IN THE DARK
© 1987 United Feature Syndicate, Inc.
OUR KEEN EYESIGHT ALLOWS US TO SEE PERFECTLY IN THE BLACKEST OF...
GOOSH!
CLICK
I THINK I'LL CURL UP AND DIE NOW
ODIE
JIM DAVIS 6-5
HERE'S SOMETHING A LITTLE DIFFERENT FOR DINNER TONIGHT, GARFIELD
GARFI
JIM DAVIS
© 1987 United Feature Syndicate, Inc.
I'M PUTTING YOU ON A HIGH-FIBER DIET
GARFIELD
GARFIELD
6-6

ARRRRGH!
© 1987 United Feature Syndicate, Inc.
GARFIELD! HOW MANY TIMES HAVE I TOLD YOU NOT TO LIE NEAR THE DOOR?!
I'M SICK OF TRIPPING OVER YOU!
ALL RIGHT! ALL RIGHT!
WHY DOES THIS ALWAYS HAPPEN TO ME?
JIM DAVIS 6-7
ARRRRGH!
HOW MANY TIMES HAVE I TOLD YOU NOT TO LIE IN THE MIDDLE OF THE LIVING ROOM?!
I CAN'T WIN

NORMALLY, I HATE ALARM CLOCKS
© 1987 United Feature Syndicate, Inc.
BUT THIS ONE I LIKE
IT'S BROKEN
JIM DAVIS 6-8
WOOAAH!
TRIP
© 1987 United Feature Syndicate, Inc.
GARFIELD! WATCH WHERE YOU'RE GOING!
WHY DON'T YOU WATCH WHERE I'M GOING?
JIM DAVIS 6-9

A SPIDER!
YIPE!
WHEW!
JIM DAVIS 6-10
© 1987 United Feature Syndicate, Inc.
OH, JON, MAY I BORROW YOUR BOOK FOR JUST A MOMENT?
WHAP!
THANK YOU SO MUCH
ANYTIME
JIM DAVIS 6-11
© 1987 United Feature Syndicate, Inc.

TELL ME, GARFIELD
IF NATURE IS GOVERNED BY SURVIVAL OF THE FITTEST...
HOW COME YOU'RE STILL AROUND?!
I STAY OUT OF DRAFTS
JIM DAVIS 6-12
© 1987 United Feature Syndicate, Inc.
JIM DAVIS 6-13
YOU'RE PATHETIC, GARFIELD
Z
GARFIELD
WHAT AM I GOING TO DO WITH YOU?
WELL, FOR STARTERS, YOU COULD OCCASIONALLY WAKE ME AND REMIND ME TO SWALLOW
HELP ME
© 1987 United Feature Syndicate, Inc.

Z
Z
Z
Z
PUNT!
© 1987 United Feature Syndicate, Inc.
Z
YAWN. I HAD THE MOST WONDERFUL DREAM LAST NIGHT
JIM DAVIS
6-14
WHUMP!

YAWN-WELL LET'S SEE WHAT KIND OF DAY TODAY IS...
CRICK
CRICK
CRICK
CRICK
CRICK CRICK
CRICK
CRICK
CRICK
IT'S A NINE CRICKER
JIM DAVIS 6-15
I COULD LOOK LIKE THIS IF I WANTED TO
JIM DAVIS 6-16
BUT, I DON'T HAVE ENOUGH HANDS

HEY, GARFIELD, YOU'RE GOING TO BE NINE YEARS OLD THIS FRIDAY
THANKS FOR REMINDING ME
AS CATS GO, YOU'RE APPROACHING THE GOLDEN YEARS
THE HECK WITH THE GOLDEN YEARS. I'M FIVE AND HOLDING
6-17
JIM DAVIS
© 1987 United Feature Syndicate, Inc.
WHAT'S THE MATTER, GARFIELD? FEELING YOUR YEARS NOW THAT YOU'RE TURNING NINE?
COME CLOSER, MY SON. I'M HAVING TROUBLE HEARING YOU
6-18
SLAP! SLAP! SLAP! SLAP!
JIM DAVIS
© 1987 United Feature Syndicate, Inc.

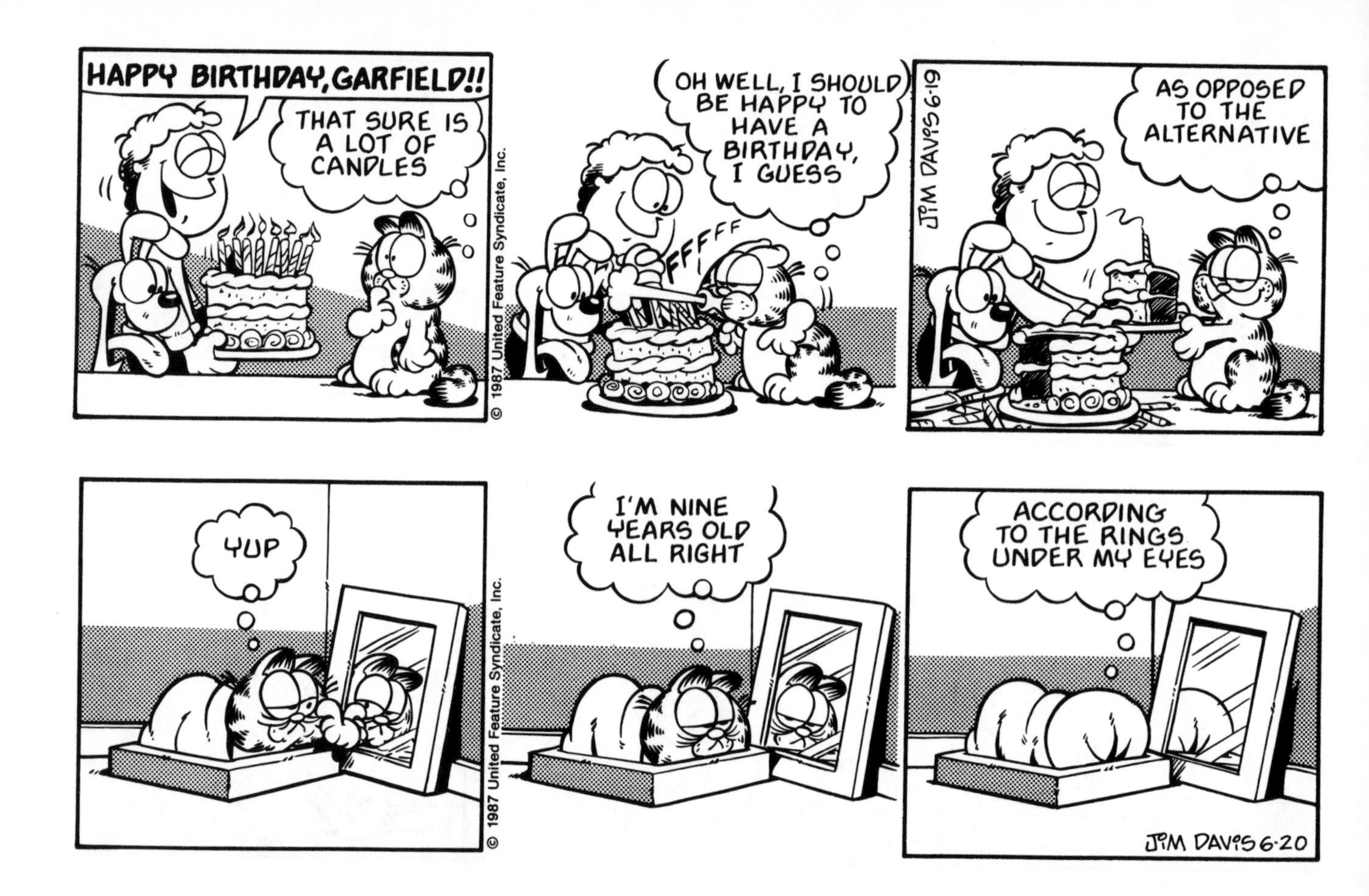
HAPPY BIRTHDAY, GARFIELD!!
THAT SURE IS A LOT OF CANDLES
© 1987 United Feature Syndicate, Inc.
FFFFFF
OH WELL, I SHOULD BE HAPPY TO HAVE A BIRTHDAY, I GUESS
JIM DAVIS 6-19
AS OPPOSED TO THE ALTERNATIVE
YUP
© 1987 United Feature Syndicate, Inc.
I'M NINE YEARS OLD ALL RIGHT
ACCORDING TO THE RINGS UNDER MY EYES
JIM DAVIS 6-20

SHAKE
SHAKE
SHAKE
SHAKE
YAWN
IT MUST HAVE BEEN SOMETHING I ATE
6-21
JIM DAVIS

JIM DAVIS 6-22
© 1987 United Feature Syndicate, Inc.
POOMP!
BLAT!
SQUIRT!
JIM DAVIS 6-23
YEEEOW!
I'M HUNGRY
SWIPE
© 1987 United Feature Syndicate, Inc.
THAT HURT!!
I'LL SAY... I THINK I BROKE A NAIL

THERE YOU GO, GARFIELD. EAT HEARTY!
JIM DAVIS 6-24
DRY CAT FOOD AND HOSE WATER
© 1987 United Feature Syndicate, Inc.
BE STILL, MY BEATING TASTE BUDS
CAT FOOD
GARFIELD, WE'RE OUT OF CAT FOOD. HOW ABOUT DOG FOOD INSTEAD?
© 1987 United Feature Syndicate, Inc.
LET ME PUT IT THIS WAY, IT'S EITHER DOG FOOD OR NOTHING
ARF
I'LL GET IT
JIM DAVIS 6-25

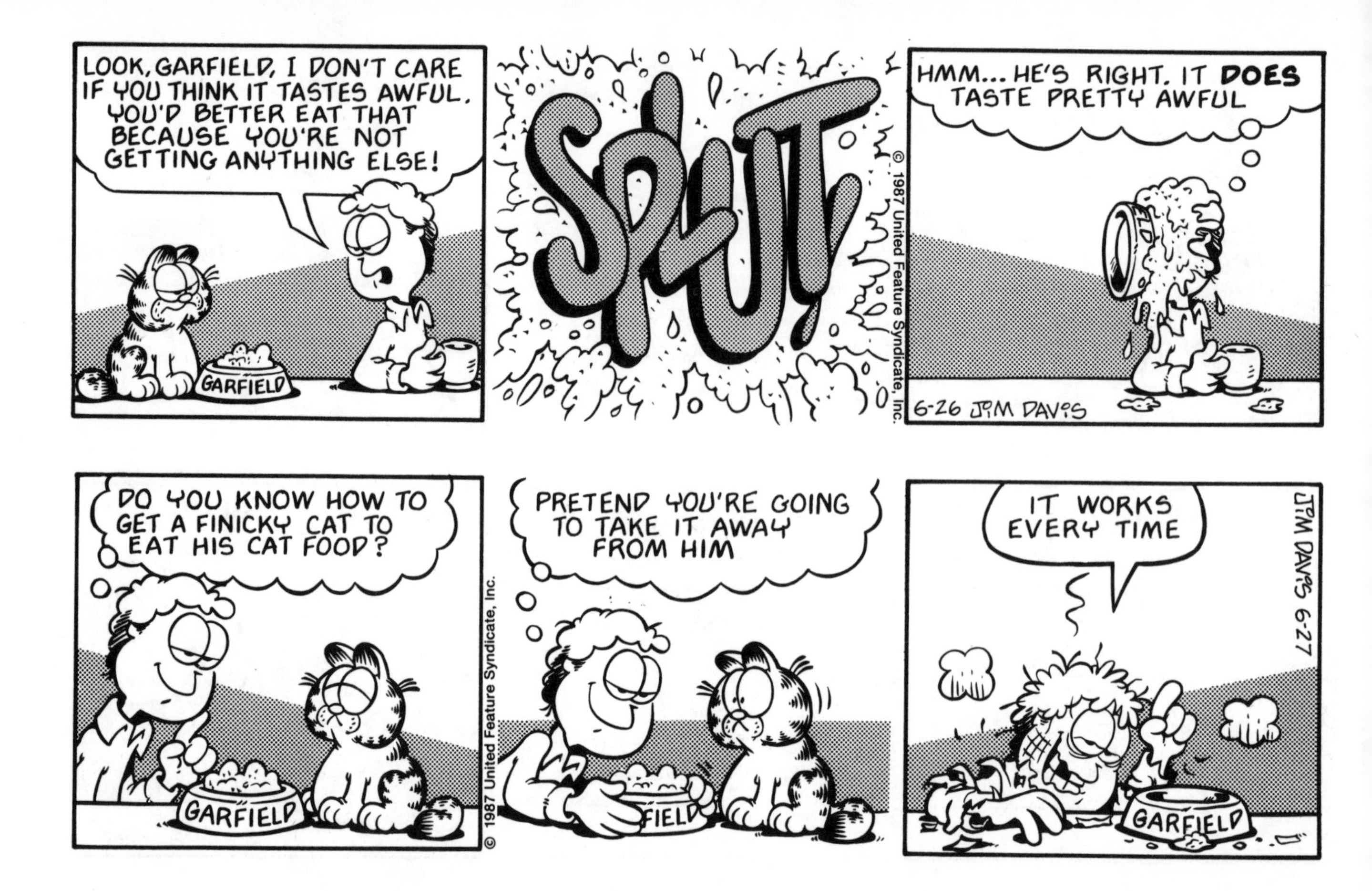
LOOK, GARFIELD, I DON'T CARE IF YOU THINK IT TASTES AWFUL. YOU'D BETTER EAT THAT BECAUSE YOU'RE NOT GETTING ANYTHING ELSE!
GARFIELD
SPLUT
© 1987 United Feature Syndicate, Inc.
HMM... HE'S RIGHT. IT **DOES** TASTE PRETTY AWFUL
6-26 JIM DAVIS
DO YOU KNOW HOW TO GET A FINICKY CAT TO EAT HIS CAT FOOD?
GARFIELD
© 1987 United Feature Syndicate, Inc.
PRETEND YOU'RE GOING TO TAKE IT AWAY FROM HIM
FIELD
IT WORKS EVERY TIME
GARFIELD
JIM DAVIS 6-27

Z
Z
© 1987 United Feature Syndicate, Inc.
SNORT. WHA?!!
GARFIELD, I'M TRYING TO SLEEP! WHAT DO YOU WANT?
WHAT EVERY OTHER CAT IN THE WORLD WANTS FROM ITS OWNER AT 3:00 A.M.
MY TEDDY BEAR!
JIM DAVIS 6-28

FLIP
FLIP
FLIP
FLIP
FLIP
JUST AS I THOUGHT, JUNE 29,1987
"THE WORLD'S LONGEST MONDAY"
© 1987 United Feature Syndicate, Inc.
JIM DAVIS 6-29
GARFIELD! YOU FIXED MY FUNNY GLASSES!
YUP
HOW DID YOU DO IT?
I USED GLUE
HEY! THEY'RE STUCK TO MY FACE!
GEE, JON, I GUESS THIS MEANS I'LL NEVER BE ABLE TO TAKE YOU SERIOUSLY AGAIN
© 1987 United Feature Syndicate, Inc.
JIM DAVIS 6-30

I'D LIKE TO BUY SOME GLUE SOLVENT
IS THIS A HOLDUP?
JIM DAVIS 7-1
NO, YOU SEE, MY CAT GLUED THESE GLASSES TO MY FACE
YOUR CAT?
© 1987 United Feature Syndicate, Inc.
SOUNDS SILLY, HUH?
NOT AT ALL... HELLO, POLICE?
FLEA SPRAY TO THE RESCUE!
© 1987 United Feature Syndicate, Inc.
SSSSSSSS
OOPS, THIS IS MY DEODORANT
GREAT, I'D HATE TO THINK I WAS OFFENDING THEM
JIM DAVIS 7-2

LOOK, GARFIELD, I BOUGHT YOU A RUBBER MOUSE
WHAT'S THAT FOR?
© 1987 United Feature Syndicate, Inc.
YOU CAN CHASE IT, TOSS IT IN THE AIR, STALK IT AND POUNCE ON IT
YES?
OH, FORGET IT
MAYBE IT PLAYS MUSIC OR SOMETHING
JIM DAVIS 7-3
RAOW! RAOW! RAOW!
YOU KNOW, I WONDER WHAT A DOG WOULD DO WITH A CAT IF IT EVER CAUGHT ONE?
© 1987 United Feature Syndicate, Inc.
SCREEEEE
OKAY, MUTT! YOU CAUGHT ME! NOW WHAT ARE YOU GOING TO DO WITH ME?!
NEXT TIME I LEAD, ALL RIGHT?
JIM DAVIS
7-4

OKAY, ODIE, NOW FOR A LESSON IN HOME PLUMBING
ALL THE WATER LINES IN THIS HOUSE ARE CONNECTED
© 1987 United Feature Syndicate, Inc.
THUSLY, IF I TURN THE HOT WATER ON HERE, THERE WILL NO LONGER BE HOT WATER IN JON'S SHOWER
JIM DAVIS 7-5
OBSERVE
YEOWWW!
SHHH
GET OFF THAT SINK!
AIN'T SCIENCE GREAT?

GULP
MUNCH
GOBBLE
SMACK
GLUB
SLURP
SNARF
GARFIELD
BURP
GARFIELD
© 1987 United Feature Syndicate, Inc.
AND PEOPLE SAY DINNER CONVERSATION IS A LOST ART
GARFIELD
7-6
JIM DAVIS
HEY, GANG, THE CAT'S AWAY!
JIM DAVIS 7-7
© 1987 United Feature Syndicate, Inc.
THAT OUGHTA MAKE'M PARANOID

I'M DEPRESSED, GARFIELD
HANG ON. I HAVE JUST THE THING
© 1987 United Feature Syndicate, Inc.
THIS SHOULD CHEER YOU UP
AND, OF COURSE, MISERY LOVES COMPANY
JIM DAVIS
7-8
PIZZA IS FRIENDLY AND BANANAS ARE FUNNY
© 1987 United Feature Syndicate, Inc.
PEACHES LOVE TO BE SQUEEZED AND PEAS OCCASIONALLY POP IN
I LOVE FOOD WITH PERSONALITY
JIM DAVIS 7-9

HEHWO, WIDDLE PUDDY TAT!
JIM DAVIS
© 1987 United Feature Syndicate, Inc.
VIS'M WIDDLE PUDDY TAT A NICEY WICEY PUDDY TAT?
7-10
EXCUSE ME WHILE NICEY WICEY PUDDY TAT TAKES A BARFY WARFY IN THE GRASSY WASSY
BYE-BYE, PUDDY TAT
© 1987 United Feature Syndicate, Inc.
THE NEXT PERSON TO TALK BABY TALK TO ME GETS HIS CLOCK CLEANED
JIM DAVIS 7-11
WHY, HEHWO WIDDLE PUDDY TAT!

ODIE
GARFIELD
© 1987 United Feature Syndicate, Inc.
IE
GARFIELD
PANT
PANT
PANT
SCRATCH
SCRATCH
PANT
HE
SCRATCH
ODIE
GARFIELD
JIM DAVIS 7-12

REMEMBER TO LOOK BOTH WAYS BEFORE CROSSING THE STREET, ODIE
© 1987 United Feature Syndicate, Inc.
SCREEE
THE POINT, OF COURSE, BEING TO SEE IF THERE ARE ANY CARS COMING
JIM DAVIS 7-13
ARE YOU READY FOR THE OPERA, STEVEN?
CLICK
© 1987 United Feature Syndicate, Inc.
LA-LA-LAAAH
WHY DID YOU CHANGE THE PROGRAM?
IT WASN'T INSULTING MY INTELLIGENCE ANYMORE
JIM DAVIS 7-14

♪
JPM DAVPS 7-15
© 1987 United Feature Syndicate, Inc.
ROWR!
GARFIELD'S SICK THIS MORNING. HE ASKED ME TO FILL IN FOR HIM
LEAVE THAT FERN ALONE! DO YOU HEAR ME?!
JPM DAVPS 7-16
GOOD HEAVENS, YOU REALLY ARE LISTENING TO ME. COULD IT BE YOU'RE STARTING TO RESPECT ME?
© 1987 United Feature Syndicate, Inc.
LET'S SEE YOU MAKE THAT LITTLE THING THAT HANGS DOWN IN THE BACK OF YOUR THROAT DANCE AROUND AGAIN!

I SAW THIS SCIENCE FICTION MOVIE LAST NIGHT ABOUT VEGETABLES WHO IMITATED OTHER LIFE-FORMS
JIM DAVIS 7-17
© 1987 United Feature Syndicate, Inc.
I TURNED IT OFF...
I WATCH TV TO ESCAPE
HEY, GARFIELD. WANNA GO RUNNING THIS MORNING?
YOU'VE GOT TO BE KIDDING
HARD BREATHING CAN CAUSE BRAIN DAMAGE
PANT PANT PANT
I REST MY CASE
© 1987 United Feature Syndicate, Inc.
JIM DAVIS 7-18

THIS COULD BE ANY REFRIGERATOR, MAYBE YOURS
DEEP WITHIN THE FROZEN WASTES IT LURKS
© 1987 United Feature Syndicate, Inc.
ANCIENT MAYONNAISE, FOSSILIZED CABBAGE, SLOWLY MUTATING OVER UNTOLD EONS, GRADUALLY ACHIEVING CONSCIOUSNESS...
UNTIL THAT TERRIBLE DAY WHEN IT IS UNLEASHED UPON AN UNSUSPECTING WORLD
THE COLESLAW THAT TIME FORGOT!
AYIEEEE!
JIM DAVIS 7-19
CUTE, GARFIELD. NOW FINISH CLEANING OUT THE REFRIGERATOR
QUIET, FOOL! YOU'LL AWAKEN THE SLEEPING SPUDS FROM THE PLANET FUNGUS

AH, A NICE SUMPTUOUS MEAL ALL ALONE...
JIM DAVIS 7-20
© 1987 United Feature Syndicate, Inc.
AND GARFIELD NOWHERE IN SIGHT
AND THAT WORRIES ME
I'M GOING TO LET YOU DECIDE WHAT TO DO TODAY, POOKY
© 1987 United Feature Syndicate, Inc.
POOMP !
NOT MUCH FOR TALK, BUT, WHAT AN IDEA MAN!
JIM DAVIS 7-21

YOU'D LOSE SOME WEIGHT IF YOU'D EXERCISE, GARFIELD
JIM DAVIS
7-22
© 1987 United Feature Syndicate, Inc.
MAYBE IF I BREATHED A LITTLE DEEPER
I'M BORED... I HATE BOREDOM
HURRY, GARFIELD! A QUILTING BEE SPECIAL IS COMING ON THE TELEVISION!
© 1987 United Feature Syndicate, Inc.
AND THEN, SOME PEOPLE REVEL IN IT
JIM DAVIS 7-23

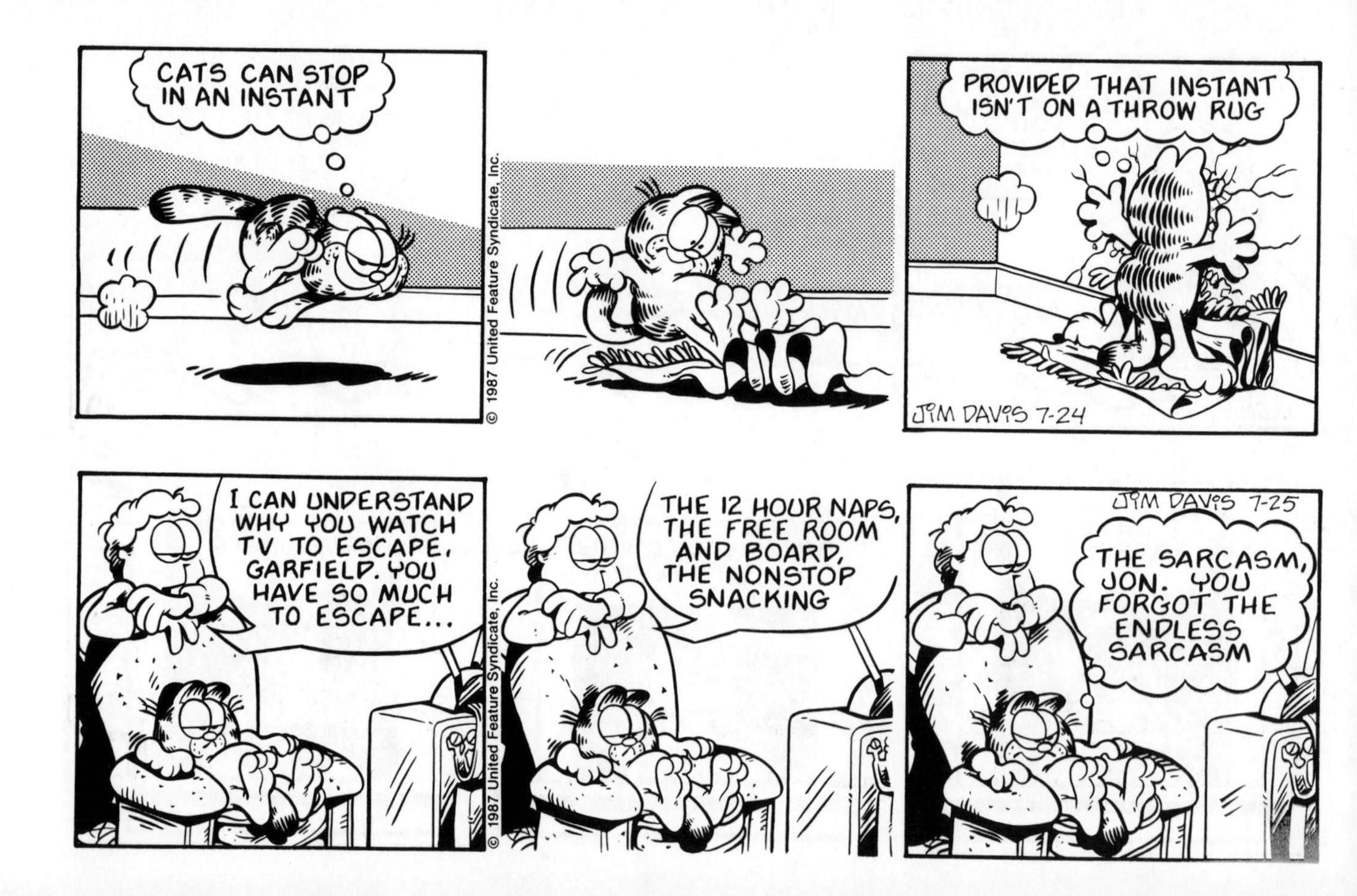
CATS CAN STOP IN AN INSTANT
PROVIDED THAT INSTANT ISN'T ON A THROW RUG
JIM DAVIS 7-24
© 1987 United Feature Syndicate, Inc.
I CAN UNDERSTAND WHY YOU WATCH TV TO ESCAPE, GARFIELD. YOU HAVE SO MUCH TO ESCAPE...
THE 12 HOUR NAPS, THE FREE ROOM AND BOARD, THE NONSTOP SNACKING
JIM DAVIS 7-25
THE SARCASM, JON. YOU FORGOT THE ENDLESS SARCASM
© 1987 United Feature Syndicate, Inc.

DO A BACK FLIP, ODIE
BEG, ODIE
ROLL OVER, ODIE
© 1987 United Feature Syndicate, Inc.
GARFIELD! DINNER!
BURP, BOY, GREAT DINNER
JIM DAVIS 7-26
NOW WHERE'S ODIE?

LET'S GO FISHING, GARFIELD
WELL, WHAT DO YOU THINK?
I THINK YOU'RE RIGHT
FISH PARALYZED BY HYSTERICAL FITS OF LAUGHTER PROBABLY **ARE** EASIER TO CATCH
© 1987 United Feature Syndicate, Inc.
JIM DAVIS 7-27
GOT MY EQUIPMENT, GOT MY FLIES. LET'S GO FISHING!
HANG ON, GARFIELD!
MY BODY IS HOOKED TO THE DRAPES
THIS IS GOING TO BE A LONG DAY
© 1987 United Feature Syndicate, Inc.
JIM DAVIS 7-28

POOR LITTLE WORMS, WAITING TO BE SKEWERED ON JON'S HOOK AND THEN FED TO SOME VICIOUS FISH. WELL IT'S NOT RIGHT!
JIM DAVIS 7-29
© 1987 United Feature Syndicate, Inc.
YOU'RE FREE! YOU'RE FREE!
SWIMMING MUST NOT BE ONE OF THEIR STRONG SUITS
REMEMBER, GARFIELD, THE KEY TO FISHING IS PATIENCE, THE ABILITY TO REMAIN MOTIONLESS FOR HOURS
GARFIELD?
© 1987 United Feature Syndicate, Inc.
Z
THAT'S MY BOY
JIM DAVIS 7-30

JIM DAVIS 7-31
WELL, GARFIELD, WHAT DO YOU THINK OF FISHING SO FAR?
© 1987 United Feature Syndicate, Inc.
I LIKE IT?
WHERE ELSE CAN YOU TAKE A THREE-HOUR NAP AND CALL IT SPORT?
I ♥
CATCH ANYTHING, BOYS?
JIM DAVIS 8-1
YEAH, BUT WE THREW 'EM BACK
© 1987 United Feature Syndicate, Inc.
THEY WERE IN DANGER OF BEING EATEN BY THE BAIT

HELLO, PLANTS
OH NO!
SHOO!
SCAT!
WELL, LET'S SEE WHAT'S ON THE MENU TODAY
MRS. BROWN! THERE'S A CAT OUT HERE!
I THINK I'LL START WITH A SALAD
NOOO!
RUN, HAROLD! RUN!
GLOMP
HAROOLD! HE GOT HAROLD!
BURP
OH, RALPH! WHAT WILL WE DO?!
STAY CALM, TAMMY. I'LL JUMP OFF THE SILL AND RUN FOR HELP!
© 1987 United Feature Syndicate, Inc.
NOW FOR DESSERT
HURRY, RALPH! HURRY!
I THINK I BROKE SOMETHING!
JIM DAVIS 8-2

LET'S GO FOR A WALK, GARFIELD. IT'S GOOD EXERCISE
JIM DAVIS
8-3
© 1987 United Feature Syndicate, Inc.
EVEN A SHORT WALK IS BETTER THAN NO WALK AT ALL
YOU'RE RIGHT
START WITH THE KITCHEN AND BACK
DONK
GARFIELD
I AM AN ARTIST
JIM DAVIS 8-4
© 1987 United Feature Syndicate, Inc.
SCHOONK!
I EAT WHAT I SEE

TAP
TAP
TAP
COOKIES
JIM DAVIS 8-5
© 1987 United Feature Syndicate, Inc.
WELL, WELL, WELL, AND JUST HOW DID YOU GET IN THERE?
COOKIES
WOULD YOU BELIEVE HOURS AND HOURS OF CAREFUL PLANNING?
COOKIES
GET UP, GARFIELD. BREAKFAST IS THE MOST IMPORTANT MEAL OF THE DAY, YOU KNOW
GARFIELD
YOU'RE QUITE RIGHT, JON. I COULDN'T AGREE WITH YOU MORE
GARFIELD
© 1987 United Feature Syndicate, Inc.
NOW, BE A GOOD BOY AND BRING IT BACK AT NOON
GARFIELD
JIM DAVIS
8-6

YOU KNOW, GARFIELD, LIFE IS LIKE A BOWL OF CHERRIES
© 1987 United Feature Syndicate, Inc.
8-7
LET DOWN YOUR GUARD, AND IT'LL GET YOU
YOU'RE GOING TO PAY FOR THIS ONE
JIM DAVIS
HEY, GARFIELD, THEY'RE DEVELOPING COMPUTERS WITH ARTIFICIAL INTELLIGENCE
BIG DEAL
© 1987 United Feature Syndicate, Inc.
I'LL BE IMPRESSED WHEN THEY INVENT ARTIFICIAL CUNNING
JIM DAVIS
8-8

CLICK!
NNNNNNG
FLIP
UNNNGH
WHAP!
SHOOP!
FLOP!
SNAP!
WHIP!
BAP!
JIM DAVIS 8-9
NO WONDER. THIS IS THE GARAGE DOOR OPENER
© 1987 United Feature Syndicate, Inc.

AHHH! COFFEE
NO! NO! DON'T DRINK IT, JON!
SHOOP!
ARRRGH! IT'S TOO LATE
Z
THAT COFFEE WAS DECAFFEINATED, YOU FOOL!
© 1987 United Feature Syndicate, Inc.
JIM DAVIS 8-10
WHAT DOES ONE HAVE TO DO TO GET ONE'S BELLY SCRATCHED AROUND HERE?
© 1987 United Feature Syndicate, Inc.
JIM DAVIS
8-11

THERE'S ONLY ONE WAY TO GET RID OF A FREE-FLOATING GUILT COMPLEX
DO SOMETHING TO DESERVE IT
JIM DAVIS 8-12
© 1987 United Feature Syndicate, Inc.
WE HUMANS ARE LUCKY, GARFIELD. WE CAN SING AND PLAY INSTRUMENTS
YOU CATS HAVE NO WAY OF SHOWING YOUR APPRECIATION FOR MUSIC
OH, BUT I DO
I SOLD YOUR PIANO
JIM DAVIS 8-13
© 1987 United Feature Syndicate, Inc.

HAVE THE LAST COOKIE, GARFIELD
I REALLY COULDN'T. YOU TAKE IT
© 1987 United Feature Syndicate, Inc.
OKAY
JIM DAVIS 8-14
YOU TWIT! DON'T YOU KNOW INSINCERE SINCERITY WHEN YOU HEAR IT?
UH-OH, IT LOOKS AS THOUGH MR. CLICHÉ IS ABOUT TO UNBURDEN HIMSELF OF ANOTHER STALE PLATITUDE
© 1987 United Feature Syndicate, Inc.
"HE WHO FILLS HIS POCKETS WITH THE ROCKS OF MISDEEDS WILL SURELY SINK IN THE RIVER OF GOOD FORTUNE"
THAT BOY WASN'T BORN, HE WAS FOUND IN A FORTUNE COOKIE
JIM DAVIS 8-15

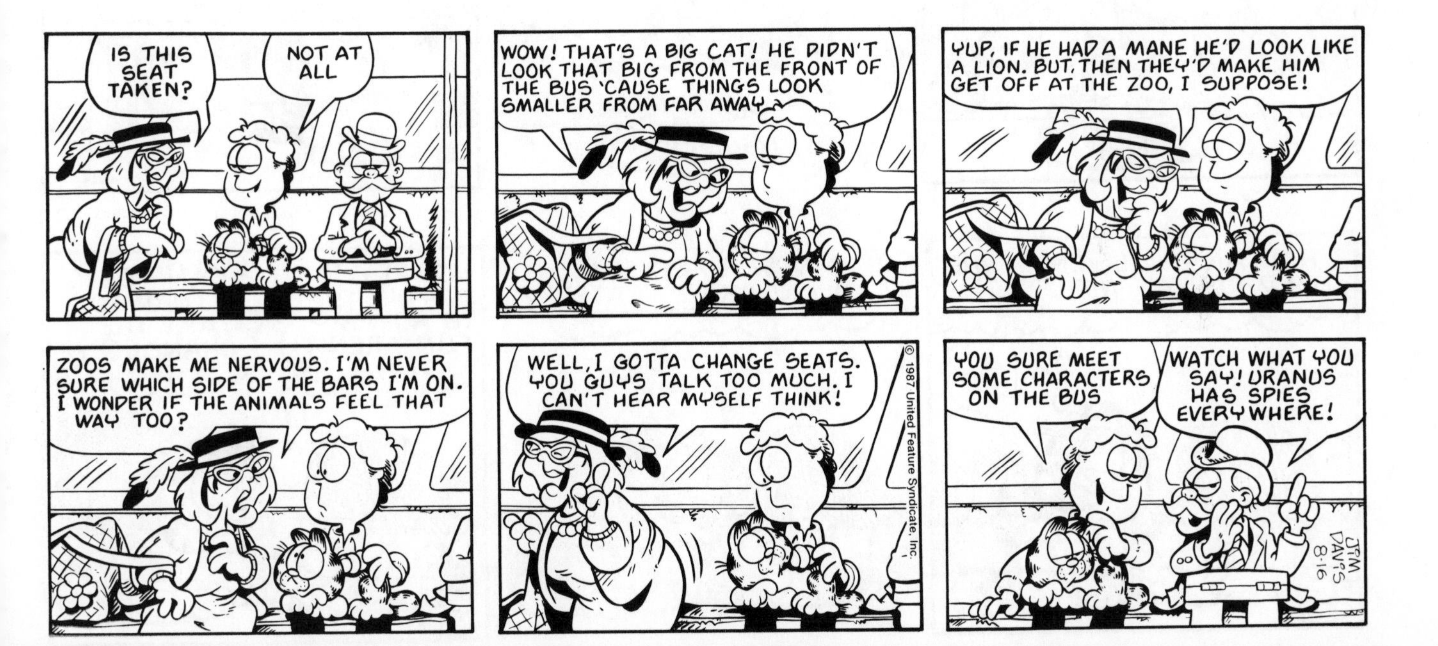
IS THIS SEAT TAKEN?
NOT AT ALL
WOW! THAT'S A BIG CAT! HE DIDN'T LOOK THAT BIG FROM THE FRONT OF THE BUS 'CAUSE THINGS LOOK SMALLER FROM FAR AWAY
YUP, IF HE HAD A MANE HE'D LOOK LIKE A LION. BUT, THEN THEY'D MAKE HIM GET OFF AT THE ZOO, I SUPPOSE!
ZOOS MAKE ME NERVOUS. I'M NEVER SURE WHICH SIDE OF THE BARS I'M ON. I WONDER IF THE ANIMALS FEEL THAT WAY TOO?
WELL, I GOTTA CHANGE SEATS. YOU GUYS TALK TOO MUCH. I CAN'T HEAR MYSELF THINK!
© 1987 United Feature Syndicate, Inc.
YOU SURE MEET SOME CHARACTERS ON THE BUS
WATCH WHAT YOU SAY! URANUS HAS SPIES EVERYWHERE!
JIM DAVIS 8-16

GARFIELD
GARFIELD
JIM DAVIS 8-17
I HAD AN UNCLE ONCE WHO USED TO PLAY WITH YARN...
HE'S NOW A PATTERN IN AN ANGORA SWEATER
YOU'RE JUST SAYING THAT TO RUIN MY FUN, AREN'T YOU?
CAN YOU AFFORD TO TAKE THE CHANCE?
JIM DAVIS 8-18

YOU'VE GOT A PRETTY GOOD THING GOING HERE, DON'T YOU?
YUP
© 1987 United Feature Syndicate, Inc.
JON FEEDS ME, STROKES ME, CHANGES MY KITTY LITTER AND CATERS TO MY WHIMS
SO WHAT DOES **HE** GET OUT OF IT?
HE GETS TO CALL HIMSELF "MASTER"
JIM DAVIS 8-19
WITH EACH NEW DAY, A CAT'S CURIOSITY MUST BE SATISFIED ANEW
© 1987 United Feature Syndicate, Inc.
KICK
YUP, THE LAW OF GRAVITY IS STILL IN EFFECT
JIM DAVIS 8-20

DEAR HAIR BALL CAT FOOD CO., I FIND YOUR CAT FOOD GIVES MY CAT A "LONG SILKY COAT OF HAIR" AS ADVERTISED...
JIM DAVIS
HOWEVER, I THINK YOU SHOULD ADD A DISCLAIMER
8-21
© 1987 United Feature Syndicate, Inc.
"DO NOT FEED YOUR CAT MORE THAN 36 CANS A DAY."
YOU'RE WASTING YOUR LIFE AWAY, GARFIELD. YOU SHOULD BE OUT THERE...UH...
OUT THERE DOING WHATEVER IT IS YOU CATS DO
© 1987 United Feature Syndicate, Inc.
THAT'S WHAT I LIKE ABOUT BEING A CAT. OUR STANDARDS ARE LOW
JIM DAVIS 8-22

DECISIONS, DECISIONS...
GARFIELD
SHOULD I EAT FIRST AND THEN SLEEP OR SLEEP FIRST AND THEN EAT?
GARFIELD
HMM... I USUALLY EAT FIRST. MAYBE I SHOULD SLEEP FIRST FOR A CHANGE OF PACE
ON THE OTHER HAND, IF I SLEEP FIRST, ODIE MIGHT EAT MY FOOD BEFORE I WAKE UP
GARFIELD
Z
RFIELD
© 1987 United Feature Syndicate, Inc.
JIM DAVIS 8-23

STUPID PET DOOR!
I THOUGHT JON FIXED IT!
UNNNGH!
JIM DAVIS 8-24
© 1987 United Feature Syndicate, Inc.
JON, REMEMBER WHEN YOU THOUGHT IT WAS A GREAT IDEA TO PUT THE PET DOOR IN?
AND HOW ODIE AND I COULD COME AND GO AS WE PLEASED?
YOU GOOFED AGAIN
JIM DAVIS 8-25
© 1987 United Feature Syndicate, Inc.

JIM DAVIS 8-26
ABOUT YOUR WEIGHT, GARFIELD
© 1987 United Feature Syndicate, Inc.
YOU'RE GETTING A BIT LARGE FOR YOUR PET DOOR
DO TELL
PURRR
© 1987 United Feature Syndicate, Inc.
HOW NICE! ARE YOU RUBBING AGAINST MY LEG TO TELL ME HOW MUCH YOU LOVE ME?
OR TO TELL ME, IF I DON'T FEED YOU, YOU'LL RIP OFF MY FACE?
BINGO!
JIM DAVIS 8-27

...AND I WAS WONDERING IF YOU'D GO OUT WITH ME TONIGHT?
8-28
YOU SAY YOU'D RATHER GO OUT WITH CAMEL SPITTLE?
ZAP HER BACK! ZAP HER BACK!
JIM DAVIS
"BUT WHAT IF YOUR BROTHER ALREADY HAS PLANS?" THAT'S WHAT I SHOULD HAVE SAID!
OL' LIGHTNING WIT STRIKES AGAIN
© 1987 United Feature Syndicate, Inc.
WHIRRRRRRR
JIM DAVIS 8-29
WHIRRRRRRR
WHIRRRRRRR
I LOVE DRIVING ODIE UP THE WALL
© 1987 United Feature Syndicate, Inc.

© 1987 United Feature Syndicate, Inc.
YANK
WHIRRRR
WHIRRRRR
JIM DAVIS 8-30

THERE'S ONE THING I CAN COUNT ON FROM GARFIELD
NICE DRAPES, ARBUCKLE. IT WOULD BE A SHAME IF SOMEONE SLASHED 'EM INTO PARTY STREAMERS
© 1986 United Feature Syndicate, Inc.
PROTECTION
JIM DAVIS 8-31
I WONDER HOW GARFIELD WOULD HANDLE AN EMERGENCY?
Z
FIRE!
© 1986 United Feature Syndicate, Inc.
I GUESS I SHOULDN'T BE SURPRISED
JIM DAVIS 9-1

HURRY, GARFIELD! GET TO THE CAR!
© 1986 United Feature Syndicate, Inc.
QUICK! LOCK THE DOORS! ROLL UP THE WINDOWS!
THEY'RE PROBABLY WATCHING THE HOUSE RIGHT NOW. WE'LL HAVE TO MOVE OUT OF STATE!
HE USED AN EXPIRED COUPON
JIM DAVIS 9-2
AH, IT'S SO NICE TO OWN A CAT
© 1986 United Feature Syndicate, Inc.
OWN? NOBODY **OWNS** A CAT
JIM DAVIS 9-3
BUT YOU MAY THINK OF ME AS ON LONG-TERM LOAN

LEAVE THAT STATION ON, GARFIELD. IT'S "HAMLET"
TO BE OR NOT TO BE
CLICK!
HEY! WHAT ARE YOU DOING?!
SOLVING AN EXISTENTIAL DILEMMA WITH MODERN TECHNOLOGY
© 1986 United Feature Syndicate, Inc.
JIM DAVIS 9-4
I FEEL LIKE LETTING MY BETTER NATURE SHOW THROUGH TODAY
PUNT!
MY WORSE NATURE IS NOT A PRETTY SIGHT
© 1986 United Feature Syndicate, Inc.
9-5 JIM DAVIS

THAT'S RIGHT, BEVERLY, I WILL NOT GO OUT WITH YOU TONIGHT
YES, I KNOW YOU'RE MADLY IN LOVE WITH ME, BUT, I HAVE BETTER THINGS TO DO
NOW, NOW, BEVERLY, YOU KNOW I HATE IT WHEN YOU GROVEL, AND STOP SOBBING UNCONTROLLABLY
AT THE SOUND OF THE TONE THE TIME WILL BE 10:00 A.M.
© 1987 United Feature Syndicate, Inc.
JIM DAVIS 9-6
BEEP
YOU MONSTER, HOW DARE YOU BREAK THAT COMPUTER'S HEART?
OH, SHUT UP

JIM DAVIS 9-7
AH-AH-AH
© 1987 United Feature Syndicate, Inc.
CHOO
BLESS YOU
LET'S HEAR IT FOR SLEEP!
© 1987 United Feature Syndicate, Inc.
GIMME A "Z"!
Z
JIM DAVIS 9-8

JUST LOOK AT THE SMILE ON GARFIELD'S FACE

Z

HE MUST BE HAVING A GREAT DREAM

Z

Z

Z

JIM DAVIS 9-9

P-THB-THB-THB-THB!

P-THB THB

LOOK, ODIE! I CAN TOUCH MY NOSE WITH MY TONGUE!
CAN YOU DO THAT?
© 1987 United Feature Syndicate, Inc.
JIM DAVIS 9-11
SLEEP IS WONDERFUL
WHAT WOULD PEOPLE BE WITHOUT SLEEP?
REAL TIRED, PROBABLY
© 1987 United Feature Syndicate, Inc.
JIM DAVIS 9-12

HEY, GARFIELD. I'VE NOTICED YOU'RE PRETTY OUT OF SHAPE
NONSENSE, I WATCH 30 MINUTES OF AEROBICS A DAY
9-13
SO I BOUGHT YOU THESE JOGGING SHOES!
I HOPE YOU KEPT THE RECEIPT
JIM DAVIS
SEE? THESE SHOES ARE BUILT TO ABSORB SHOCKS
WHACK!
HE'S RIGHT. I BARELY FELT THAT
© 1987 United Feature Syndicate, Inc.
THE SHOES, WHERE ARE THEY?
LAST I SAW 'EM, THEY WERE JOGGING TO THE GARBAGE DISPOSAL

© 1987 United Feature Syndicate, Inc.
9-14
JIM DAVIS
SURPRISE, GARFIELD! WON'T THIS BE FUN TO PLAY IN?
TAKE IT BACK
© 1987 United Feature Syndicate, Inc.
JIM DAVIS 9-15
THERE'S NO ELEVATOR

ODIE IS VERY SPECIAL
HE WAS BRED TO BE A WORKING DOG
SPECIFICALLY, A PAPERWEIGHT OR A DOORSTOP
JIM DAVIS 9-16
© 1987 United Feature Syndicate, Inc.
GARFIELD, YOU'VE LOST WEIGHT!
I DON'T BELIEVE IT!
JIM DAVIS 9-17
© 1987 United Feature Syndicate, Inc.

GARFIELD, YOU EAT TOO MUCH JUNK FOOD. EAT SOMETHING GOOD FOR YOU
ZAP... YOU'RE A CARROT STICK
JIM DAVIS 9-18
GREAT CHEFS KNOW IT'S THE APPEARANCE OF FOOD THAT COUNTS
GUP!
BUT, GREAT EATERS KNOW IT'S THE AMOUNT OF FOOD THAT COUNTS
JIM DAVIS 9-19

WHUMP!
HAW! HAW!
HAW! HAW!
ZIP!
WHUMP!
HAW! HAW!
HAW!
REBA! COME HERE AND LOOK AT THIS, BUT YOU'D BETTER CINCH UP YOUR CORSET FIRST!
© 1987 United Feature Syndicate, Inc.
JIM DAVIS 9-20

JIM DAVIS 9-21
ARE YOU EVER SERIOUS, GARFIELD?
I GUESS NOT
© 1987 United Feature Syndicate, Inc.
IT'S HARD TO BE SERIOUS WHEN YOU'RE NAKED!
YAWN
JIM DAVIS 9-22
YAWN... BOREDOM IS CONTAGIOUS
© 1987 United Feature Syndicate, Inc.
OH NO! SO'S STUPIDITY

SEND TO: ACME LASAGNA FACTORY
SEND TO: ACME LASAGNA FACTORY
© 1987 United Feature Syndicate, Inc.
NOT ENOUGH POSTAGE, GARFIELD
RATS
SEND TO: ACME LASAGNA FACTORY
JIM DAVIS 9-23
GET READY TO HAVE SOME MAJOR YUCKS, YOU GUYS
JIM DAVIS 9-24
SMILE MOUTHS!
© 1987 United Feature Syndicate, Inc.
HEE HEE!
I'LL KEEP HIM LAUGHING WHILE YOU GET THE AUTHORITIES

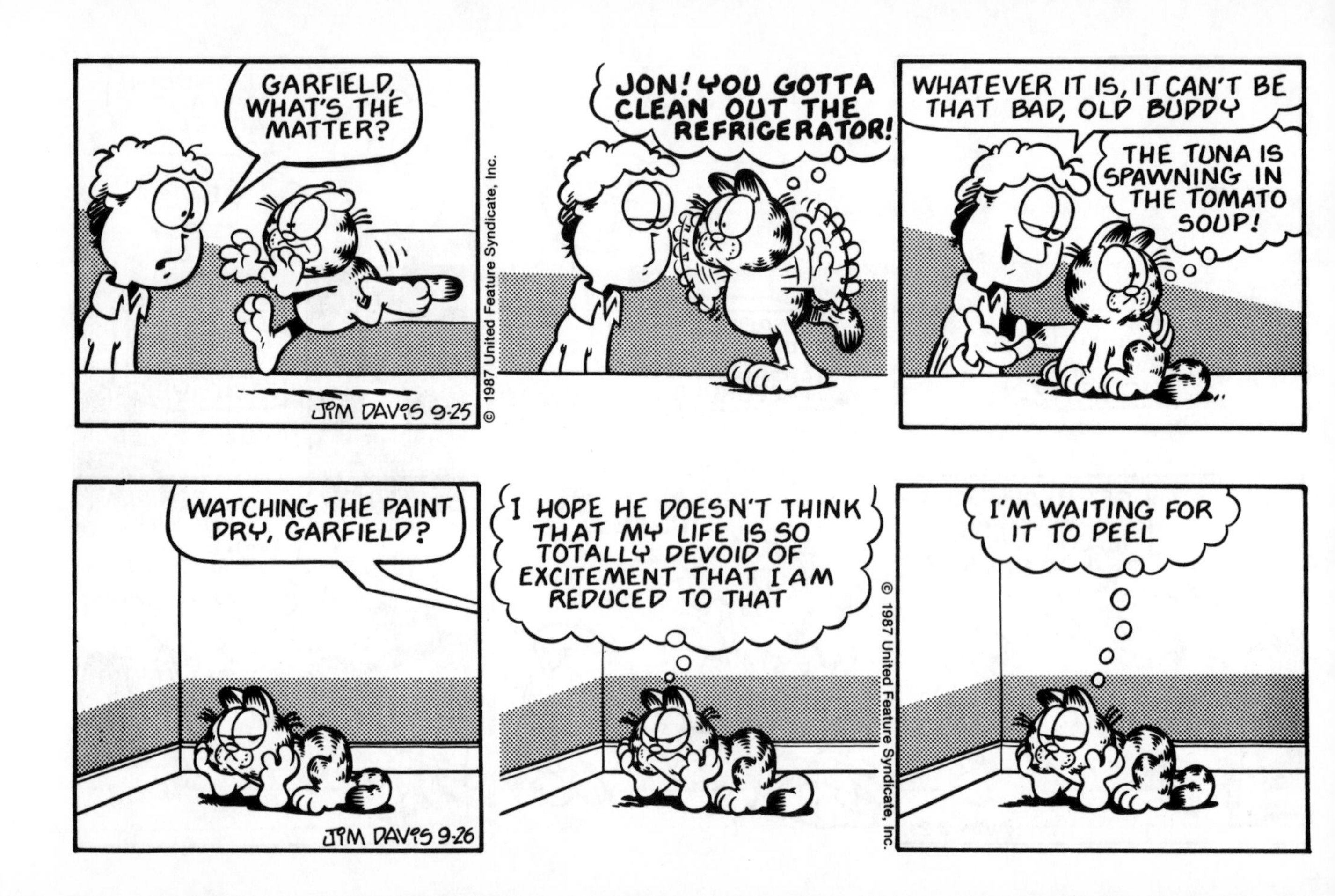
GARFIELD, WHAT'S THE MATTER?
JIM DAVIS 9-25
© 1987 United Feature Syndicate, Inc.
JON! YOU GOTTA CLEAN OUT THE REFRIGERATOR!
WHATEVER IT IS, IT CAN'T BE THAT BAD, OLD BUDDY
THE TUNA IS SPAWNING IN THE TOMATO SOUP!
WATCHING THE PAINT DRY, GARFIELD?
JIM DAVIS 9-26
I HOPE HE DOESN'T THINK THAT MY LIFE IS SO TOTALLY DEVOID OF EXCITEMENT THAT I AM REDUCED TO THAT
© 1987 United Feature Syndicate, Inc.
I'M WAITING FOR IT TO PEEL

A HUNGRY VULTURE PERCHES ABOVE HIS PREY, SILENTLY, PATIENTLY, WAITING FOR HIS MEAL TO DRAW ITS LAST BREATH
CLICK
CLICK
STOP THAT! YOU KNOW I HATE THAT!
NO MORE VULTURES!
NO MORE VULTURES
JIM DAVIS
9-27
© 1987 United Feature Syndicate, Inc.
Z
A VORACIOUS ALLIGATOR STEALTHILY GLIDES TOWARD THE FINGERS OF AN UNWARY RIVER TRAVELER

NOTHING IS SHOWING UP ON THE COMPUTER RADAR SO I'LL PUT A NICE "MR. SUNSHINE" RIGHT HERE
JIM DAVIS 9-28
BUT, SATELLITE PICTURES SHOW AN APPROACHING LOW-PRESSURE AREA, SO I'LL PUT MEAN OL' "MR. THUNDERSTORM" AND HIS LIGHTNING BOLT RIGHT HERE
© 1987 United Feature Syndicate, Inc.
LOOK OUT, MR. SUNSHINE! BOOM! KABOOM! BLAM!
MILLIONS IN STATE-OF-THE-ART ELECTRONIC EQUIPMENT TO GATHER DATA, AND WE GET BABY TALK
LET'S CHECK THE WEATHER
© 1987 United Feature Syndicate, Inc.
HMM. LOOKS LIKE A GOOD DAY TO STAY IN BED
MOSTLY BORING THIS MORNING WITH A 50% CHANCE OF INTERMITTENT DEPRESSION THIS AFTERNOON
JIM DAVIS 9-29

DEPRESSION IS WAKING UP WITH THE UNEASY FEELING THE WORLD IS OUT TO GET YOU
ZOOM
AND FINDING OUT YOU'RE RIGHT
JIM DAVIS 9-30
© 1987 United Feature Syndicate, Inc.
BEING DEPRESSED IS BAD ENOUGH. NOW JON WILL PROBABLY TRY TO CHEER ME UP WITH STUPID PLATITUDES
YOU'RE DEPRESSING, GARFIELD. AND YOU'RE FAT AND LAZY TOO
THEN AGAIN, EVEN STUPID PLATITUDES HAVE THEIR GOOD POINTS
JIM DAVIS 10-1
© 1987 United Feature Syndicate, Inc.

CHEER UP, GARFIELD. JUST REMEMBER THAT LIFE IS JUST A GAME
IT'S NOT WHETHER YOU WIN OR LOSE, BUT HOW YOU PLAY THAT COUNTS
SO, WHAT ARE YOU GOING TO DO TODAY?
FORFEIT
JIM DAVIS 10-2
© 1987 United Feature Syndicate, Inc.
I HATE THOSE LITTLE INSERT CARDS
CAT WORLD
JIM DAVIS 10-3
SHAKE
SHAKE
SHAKE
© 1987 United Feature Syndicate, Inc.
JUST AS I SUSPECTED

THAT STUPID DOG NEXT DOOR IS IN FOR A BIG SURPRISE
WHEN HE COMES BY, HE WILL MISTAKE THE MIRROR FOR ME
© 1987 United Feature Syndicate, Inc.
THEN HE WILL ATTACK AND FALL INTO THIS PIT
THEN THIS NET WILL FALL ON HIM
THEN THIS CEMENT MIXER WILL TIP, SEALING THAT SUCKER UP FOR ABOUT TEN MILLION YEARS
WAIT! WAIT! GO BACK AND COME IN AGAIN!
JIM DAVIS 10-4

DO YOU ALWAYS INSULT THE PEOPLE YOU WEIGH?
YES. IT'S A DEFENSE MECHANISM
INSULTS COMPENSATE FOR MY OWN DEPRESSIONS, MY INSECURITIES, MY LOATHING FOR THIS JOB AND MY LOT IN LIFE
© 1987 United Feature Syndicate, Inc.
I'M SORRY TO HEAR THAT
THANKS, BLUBBER BOTTOM
JIM DAVIS
10-5
JIM DAVIS 10-6
© 1987 United Feature Syndicate, Inc.

CAN WE TAKE A 50-MILE HIKE TODAY, JON?
© 1987 United Feature Syndicate, Inc.
HUH? CAN WE? CAN WE? CAN WE?
BOING BOING
JIM DAVIS
YOU'RE DRINKING TOO MUCH COFFEE, GARFIELD
OR A SWIM. WHAT IF WE SWIM TO TAHITI?
10-7
JIM DAVIS 10-8
RATS!
I GIVE UP!
© 1987 United Feature Syndicate, Inc.
I'M JUST NO GOOD WITH PLANTS
AND THESE WERE THE PLASTIC ONES

I TOLD THE WOMAN AT THE FLOWER SHOP I WAS TIRED OF YOU EATING MY PLANTS
JIM DAVIS 10-9
SHE SAID YOU WOULDN'T HARM THIS ONE
© 1987 United Feature Syndicate, Inc.
BUT, I DOUBT IT
HOW MUCH DO I WEIGH TODAY, RX-2?
© 1987 United Feature Syndicate, Inc.
YOU WEIGH SOMEWHERE BETWEEN SEVEN AND THIRTY-TWO POUNDS
I HAVE LEARNED IT IS WISE TO GIVE MY CUSTOMERS A WIDE SELECTION
JIM DAVIS
10-10

WATCH ME BLOW THIS BUBBLE. YOU'RE GOING TO GET A BANG OUT OF IT
FUH- FUH- FUH- FUH
BANG
YOU'RE RIGHT. THAT WAS FUN
© 1987 United Feature Syndicate, Inc.
HERE! YOU CHEW THE GUM THIS TIME!
THAT'S IT, FELLA. BLOW IT BIG!
FUH-FUH
BANG
IT'S ALL IN THE LIPS
10-11
JIM DAVIS

HMM, MY HOROSCORE SAYS I'M GOING TO BE VISITED BY AN OLD ACQUAINTANCE TODAY
SPLUT
UNCANNY
JIM DAVIS 10-12
© 1987 United Feature Syndicate, Inc.
HA! MISSED ME!
JIM DAVIS 10-13
SPLUT!
WHOA...BOOMERANG SPLUTS
© 1987 United Feature Syndicate, Inc.

© 1987 United Feature Syndicate, Inc.
SPLUT!
JIM DAVIS 10-14
SPLUT
© 1987 United Feature Syndicate, Inc.
CLANK!
THEY MUST BE RUNNING OUT OF AMMO!
JIM DAVIS 10-15

GOURMANDS KNOW THEIR UTENSILS. THIS IS THE TABLE-SPOON, THE TEASPOON, THE SOUPSPOON, THE SUGAR SPOON
GARFIEL
JIM DAVIS 10-16
© 1987 United Feature Syndicate, Inc.
AND MY PERSONAL FAVORITE...
GARFIELD
THE PLAY SPOON!
SPLUT!
TOING
GARFIELD
GARFIELD, WHY DO YOU ALWAYS SPIT THE CHERRY PITS OUT ONTO THE TABLE?
POO
JIM DAVIS 10-17
© 1987 United Feature Syndicate, Inc.
I LIKE A LITTLE FLOOR SHOW AFTER DINNER

OH-NO! SOMEONE ATE MY DINNER!
GARFIELD
AHA! FAT MICE!
© 1987 United Feature Syndicate, Inc.
JIM DAVIS 10-18
YOU GUYS WOULDN'T KNOW WHAT HAPPENED TO MY DINNER, WOULD YOU?
OH, SURE! BLAME US
IT'S ALWAYS THE MICE'S FAULT, RIGHT MEN?
NOT EVEN A FAIR TRIAL
TYRANT!
ALL RIGHT! I'M SORRY I MENTIONED IT
WELL I SHOULD HOPE SO!
I HOPE THEY EXPLODE
YEAH! AND NEXT TIME EASE UP ON THE TACO SAUCE!

YAWN
AHH...THERE'S NOTHING LIKE A GOOD NAP
© 1987 United Feature Syndicate, Inc.
WITH THE POSSIBLE EXCEPTION OF TWO GOOD NAPS
JIM DAVIS 10-19
THE COFFEE'S STRONG TODAY
© 1987 United Feature Syndicate, Inc.
SLAP
SLAP
SLAP
SLAP
SLAP
NOT ONLY STRONG, BUT MEAN!
JIM DAVIS 10-20

FOOD! HOW DO I LOVE THEE? LET ME COUNT THE WAYS...
GARFIELD
1, 2, 3, 4, 5 ...
GARFIELD
ARE N'T YOU GOING TO EAT, GARFIELD?
5,743, 5,744...
GARFIELD
JIM DAVIS 10-21
© 1987 United Feature Syndicate, Inc.
Z
GARFIELD
GARFIELD!
GARFIELD
FALL ASLEEP IN YOUR FOOD AGAIN?
DON'T ASK STUPID QUESTIONS. JUST GET THE CHISEL
JIM DAVIS 10-22
© 1987 United Feature Syndicate, Inc.

JIM DAVIS
© 1987 United Feature Syndicate, Inc.
SIGH
10-23
IN THE MORNING, THERE'S NOTHING I ENJOY MORE THAN A GOOD CUP OF COFFEE
© 1987 United Feature Syndicate, Inc.
AS I WAS SAYING...
JIM DAVIS 10-24

YOU SEE, RENEE, I'M A PRETTY MATURE, SUAVE KINDA GUY
© 1987 United Feature Syndicate, Inc.
ARE THESE YOURS?
HEH, HEH. WELL...UH
THEY HAVE TEDDY BEARS ALL OVER THEM
WHAT'S THIS? A CERTIFICATE OF ACHIEVEMENT FROM "THUMB SUCKERS ANONYMOUS"
GARFIELD!
JPM DAVIS 10-25
BUNNY SLIPPERS?

THIS HONEY HAS LOTS OF OPTIONS LIKE WINDSHIELD WIPERS AND A HORN
USED CARS
YOU MEAN THINGS LIKE WINDSHIELD WIPERS AND A HORN ARE OPTIONS?
NO OFFENSE, PAL, BUT IN YOUR PRICE RANGE, THE **TIRES** ARE OPTIONAL
JIM DAVIS 10-26
© 1987 United Feature Syndicate, Inc.
THIS CAR'S A REAL STEAL AT $1,900
HONEST ED'S USED CARS
E-Z CREDIT
JIM DAVIS 10-27
IT HAS TWICE THE LUGGAGE SPACE OF ANY OTHER CAR IN ITS CLASS
HONEST ED'S USED CARS
E-Z CREDIT
© 1987 United Feature Syndicate, Inc.
WHERE'S THE BACK SEAT?
OH, NO! I'LL NOTIFY THE AUTHORITIES
HONEST ED'S USED CARS
E-Z CREDIT

HONEST ED'S USED CARS
DON'T GO AWAY, FOLKS, I'LL BE RIGHT BACK
© 1987 United Feature Syndicate, Inc.
HONEST ED SEEMS NICE ENOUGH, GARFIELD, BUT THERE'S SOMETHING ABOUT HIM I DON'T TRUST
MAYBE IT'S THE FACT HIS OFFICE IS IN A PICKUP TRUCK WITH THE ENGINE RUNNING
JIM DAVIS 10-28
NICE DOIN' BUSINESS WITH YOU. AND, REMEMBER, AT HONEST ED'S, WE STAND BESIDE EVERY CAR WE SELL
DON'T YOU MEAN YOU STAND "BEHIND" EVERY CAR YOU SELL?
© 1987 United Feature Syndicate, Inc.
JIM DAVIS 10-29
NOT WITH THE MECHANICS I'VE GOT WORKING FOR ME!
CRASH
VAROOM!

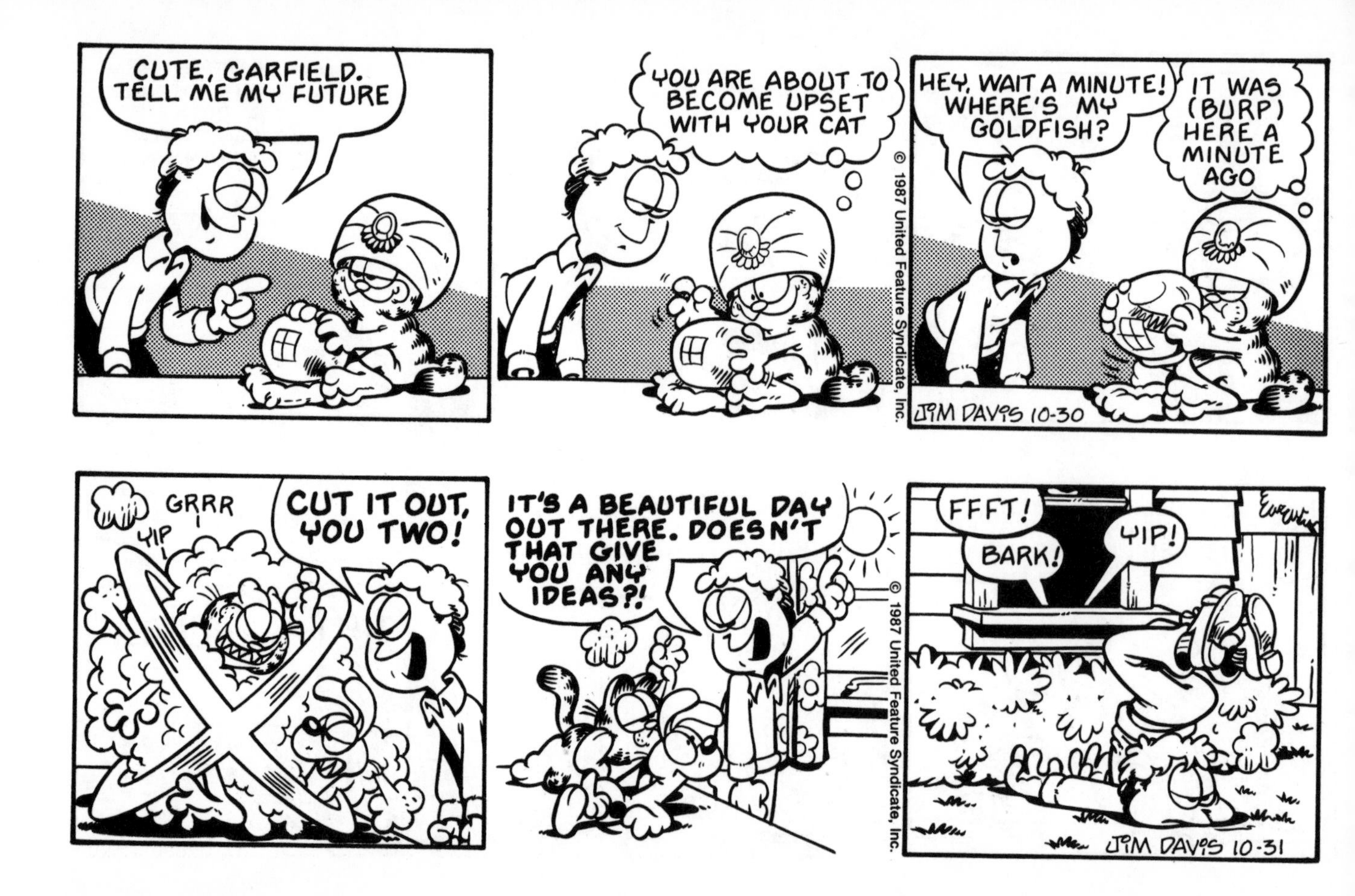
CUTE, GARFIELD. TELL ME MY FUTURE
YOU ARE ABOUT TO BECOME UPSET WITH YOUR CAT
HEY, WAIT A MINUTE! WHERE'S MY GOLDFISH?
IT WAS (BURP) HERE A MINUTE AGO
© 1987 United Feature Syndicate, Inc.
JIM DAVIS 10-30
GRRR
YIP
CUT IT OUT, YOU TWO!
IT'S A BEAUTIFUL DAY OUT THERE. DOESN'T THAT GIVE YOU ANY IDEAS?!
FFFT!
BARK!
YIP!
© 1987 United Feature Syndicate, Inc.
JIM DAVIS 10-31

KNEAD
KNEAD
KNEAD
Z
Z
© 1987 United Feature Syndicate, Inc.
OH, NO!! MY QUILT!
11-1
OH, WELL... I SUPPOSE I SHOULDN'T YELL AT HIM...
HE'S JUST DOING WHAT COMES NATURALLY FOR A CA-
JIM DAVIS
GARFIELD!

IS THAT TODAY'S MAIL, GARFIELD?
YO
JIM DAVIS 11-2
© 1987 United Feature Syndicate, Inc.
HERE ARE YOUR PERSONAL LETTERS, BILLS AND CATALOGS
AND "INSTANT MILLIONAIRE" GIVEAWAYS
YOU'RE LAZY, GARFIELD
YOU JUST DON'T UNDERSTAND, DO YOU, JON?
© 1987 United Feature Syndicate, Inc.
IN THE GRAND SCHEME OF THINGS, EACH OF US HAS OUR LITTLE NICHE TO FILL
THROUGH WITH OUR RATIONALIZATION, ARE WE?
IT'S MY NICHE TIME
JIM DAVIS 11-3

MORNIN' HON. THE USUAL?
YOU GOT IT, IRMA
© 1987 United Feature Syndicate, Inc.
JIM DAVIS 11-4
SAY, HON. WHAT **IS** THE USUAL?
I WAS HOPING YOU'D KNOW
THESE PEOPLE ARE IN DESPERATE TROUBLE
TRY THIS NEW HEALTH FOOD FOR CATS, GARFIELD. IT HAS EXTRA FIBER
RFIELD
BLUT
GARFIELD
© 1987 United Feature Syndicate, Inc.
JUST AS I SUSPECTED
JIM DAVIS 11-5

WAKE UP, GARFIELD
I CAN'T MOVE. MY BATTERY IS DEAD
SNIFF...HANG ON! I THINK I SMELL A JUMP START COMING MY WAY!
© 1987 United Feature Syndicate, Inc.
JIM DAVIS 11-6
HEY, GARFIELD, I LOOKED UP THE WORD "LAZY" IN THE DICTIONARY AND THEY HAD YOUR PICTURE BY IT
THAT'S A LIE
I SLEPT THROUGH THE APPOINTMENT FOR THE PHOTO SESSION
© 1987 United Feature Syndicate, Inc.
JIM DAVIS 11-7

POTATO CHIPS!
CHIPS
BIGGER
WHY DO THEY MAKE THESE BAGS SO HARD TO OPEN?
CHIPS
BIG
© 1987 United Feature Syndicate, Inc.
EERRRGGHH
11-8
NNGGNNFF
SQUEEZE
CHIPS
BIG
JIM DAVIS
KA-BLAM!
GARFIELD! WHAT HAPPENED?
THEY OUGHTA PUT WARNINGS ON THOSE BAGS!

CATS HAVE JUST SURPASSED DOGS AS THE COUNTRY'S FAVORITE PETS!
© 1987 United Feature Syndicate, Inc.
SOMEHOW THE VICTORY WOULD HAVE BEEN MORE SATISFYING HAD THE COMPETITION BEEN STIFFER
JIM DAVIS 11-9
SOMETIMES I THINK I'M SLOWING DOWN
© 1987 United Feature Syndicate, Inc.
GARFIELD! DINNER!
CHOOM!
BUT, THERE'S STILL A LITTLE LIFE LEFT IN THE OL' AFTERBURNERS
GARFIELD
JIM DAVIS 11-10

GARFIELD, YOU'RE NEVER GOING TO LOSE WEIGHT EATING BETWEEN MEALS. THERE'S ONLY ONE THING TO DO
GARFIELD
JIM DAVIS 11-11
© 1987 United Feature Syndicate, Inc.
DO YOU KNOW THE MEANING OF "WILLPOWER"?
GARFIELD
I DON'T KNOW THE MEANING OF "BETWEEN MEALS"
GARFIELD

LOOK, ODIE, JON'S SLEEPING
Z
MAYBE WE SHOULD BE QUIET AND LET HIM REST
Z
© 1987 United Feature Syndicate, Inc.
OR WE CAN SHAVE HIS HEAD
Z
JIM DAVIS 11-12

HEY, GARFIELD, I HAVE A NEW CAT FOOD FOR YOU
COME ON, GIVE IT A TRY. IT'S NOT THAT BAD
I DON'T KNOW, JON
RFIELD
SOMETHING TELLS ME IT ISN'T THAT GOOD
GARFIELD
JIM DAVIS 11-13
© 1987 United Feature Syndicate, Inc.
LIFE IS FILLED WITH OPPORTUNITIES
POP
SHAKE
SHAKE
SHAKE
SHAKE
PSSSSH!
IF YOU KNOW WHERE TO LOOK FOR THEM
JIM DAVIS 11-14
© 1987 United Feature Syndicate, Inc.

GARFIELD, YOU MUST BE THE SLOWEST, LAZIEST THING ON THE FACE OF THE EARTH
ON THE CONTRARY
© 1987 United Feature Syndicate, Inc.
I'M NOT SLOW AT EVERYTHING I DO
GARFIELD
I'M THE FASTEST EATER I KNOW
GOOSH!
GARFIELD
I CAN FALL ASLEEP IN AN INSTANT...
PLOP
SLURP!
POMP!
AND I HAVE A LIGHTNING QUICK TEMPER
11-15
JIM DAVIS

I'VE REALLY GOT TO STOP THIS OVEREATING
GARFIELD
© 1987 United Feature Syndicate, Inc.
GARFIELD
HOW ABOUT THAT? I DIDN'T THINK I COULD DO IT
GARFIELD
JIM DAVIS 11-16
DINNER IS...
GARFIELD
© 1987 United Feature Syndicate, Inc.
WHOMP!
JIM DAVIS 11-17
SNERVED
GARFIELD

WHAT'S THE MATTER, GARFIELD? DON'T YOU FEEL GOOD?
THAT'S AN UNDERSTATEMENT
GARFIELD
DO YOU THINK IT WAS SOMETHING YOU ATE?
NO...
GARFIELD
© 1987 United Feature Syndicate, Inc.
WHANG!!
IT WAS SOMETHING **YOU** FED ME!
GARFIELD
JIM DAVIS 11-18
IT SAYS THIS CAT FOOD IS "FIT FOR A KING"
GARFIELD
© 1987 United Feature Syndicate, Inc.
RFIELD
JIM DAVIS 11-19
THE "KING'S" FOOD TASTER
GARFIELD

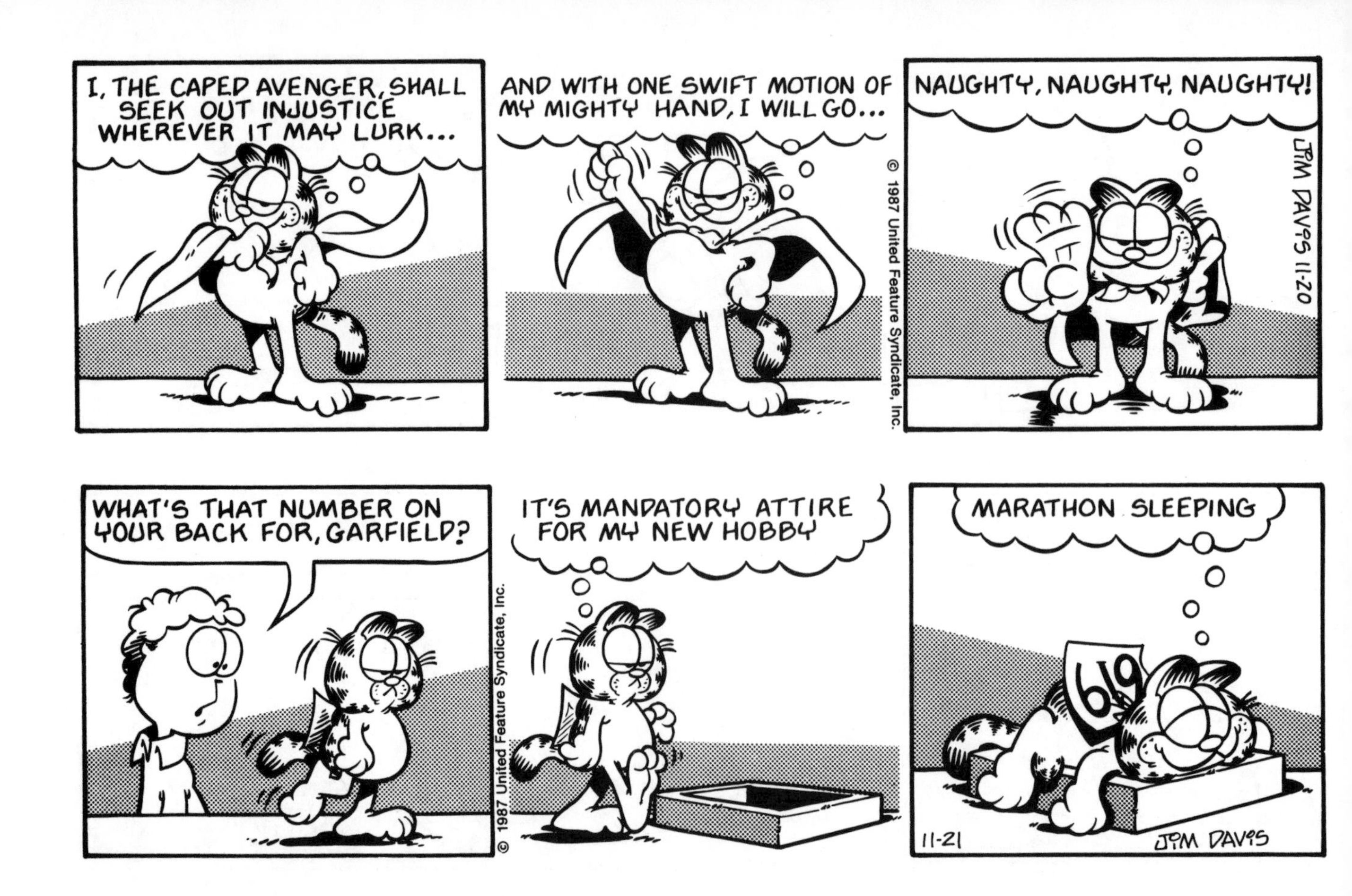

I, THE CAPED AVENGER, SHALL SEEK OUT INJUSTICE WHEREVER IT MAY LURK...
AND WITH ONE SWIFT MOTION OF MY MIGHTY HAND, I WILL GO...
NAUGHTY, NAUGHTY, NAUGHTY!
JIM DAVIS 11-20
© 1987 United Feature Syndicate, Inc.
WHAT'S THAT NUMBER ON YOUR BACK FOR, GARFIELD?
IT'S MANDATORY ATTIRE FOR MY NEW HOBBY
MARATHON SLEEPING
619
11-21
JIM DAVIS
© 1987 United Feature Syndicate, Inc.

BOY, AM I IN A ROTTEN MOOD
OUT OF MY WAY, BRIE BREATH!
PUNT!
HEY, YOU! YOU CAN'T DO THAT OR I'LL TELL MY SISTER, LORETTA!
LORETTA?
© 1987 United Feature Syndicate, Inc.
SHE'LL POUND YOU FLAT!
BRING HER ON. A GOOD FIGHT MIGHT CHEER ME UP
JIM DAVIS 11-22
HEY, LORETTA!
AAAARRRGH

JIM DAVIS 11-23
YAWN
SPLASH
SPLASH
YOU KNOW IT'S MONDAY WHEN YOU WAKE UP AND FIND SIX CRICKETS DOING A WATER BALLET IN YOUR BOWL
© 1987 United Feature Syndicate, Inc.
JIM DAVIS 11-24
MUNCH
MUNCH
MUNCH
DON'T YOU THINK YOU'VE EATEN ENOUGH WATERMELON, GARFIELD?
WHY, NO
WHY DO YOU ASK?
PTOO!
© 1987 United Feature Syndicate, Inc.

© 1987 United Feature Syndicate, Inc.
JIM DAVIS 11-25
KICK!
© 1987 United Feature Syndicate, Inc.
I'M SORRY GARFIELD. I DIDN'T SEE YOU SITTING...
JIM DAVIS 11-26
THERE

Z
JIM DAVIS 11-27
© 1987 United Feature Syndicate, Inc.
N
GARFIELD, WHY ARE YOU SO VAIN?
JIM DAVIS 11-28
© 1987 United Feature Syndicate, Inc.
IN MY CASE, MODESTY WOULD BE UNSEEMLY IN A CAT OF SUCH BREEDING
WHERE DID I GO WRONG?

HEY, JON, LOOK WHAT I CAN DO WITH THIS GRAPE
JIM DAVIS 11-29
POO!
GUNK!
OH YEAH? WATCH THIS!
© 1987 United Feature Syndicate, Inc.
I'M NOT IMPRESSED
WATCH THIS!
OH YEAH? WATCH THIS!
VETERINARY CLINIC
WHAT THE?...
DON'T ASK

GARFIELD, YOU'VE BEEN DRINKING TOO MUCH COFFEE LATELY
THERE'S NO SUCH THING AS TOO MUCH COFFEE
JIM DAVIS 11-30
© 1987 United Feature Syndicate, Inc.
I'M WORRIED ABOUT YOU
OKAY, OKAY! I'LL CUT DOWN!
JUST GIVE ME HALF A CUP
© 1987 United Feature Syndicate, Inc.
NOW, THAT'S GOOD COFFEE!
JIM DAVIS 12-1

JIM DAVIS 12-2
© 1987 United Feature Syndicate, Inc.
TOO MUCH COFFEE, GARFIELD?
YUP YUP YUP
I MADE MY WORLD FAMOUS COFFEE THIS MORNING, GARFIELD
© 1987 United Feature Syndicate, Inc.
COME ON... IT'S NOT THAT BAD!... HAVE SOME!
OH, ALL RIGHT
BUT JUST A SMALL SLICE
JIM DAVIS 12-3

SORRY, GARFIELD, BUT WE'RE OUT OF COFFEE THIS MORNING
I NOTICED
I GUESS WE'LL JUST HAVE TO GO WITHOUT
THAT'S WHAT **YOU** THINK
WHAT ARE YOU DOING?
SUCKING ON A USED COFFEE FILTER
JIM DAVIS 12-4
© 1987 United Feature Syndicate, Inc.
MEOWYRRRRRR
MEOWYRR... MEOWYRRR
GARFIELD! WHAT ARE YOU DOING?!!
JIM DAVIS 12-5
MY AGENT COULDN'T GET ME A BOOKING ON THE FENCE
TAP
TAP
TAP
© 1987 United Feature Syndicate, Inc.

HEE,
HEE,
HEE,
HEY, GARFIELD, REMEMBER THAT TIME I WAS DRINKING ROOT BEER AND YOU MADE THAT FUNNY FACE
AND I SNORTED THE ROOT BEER RIGHT OUT MY NOSE?
© 1987 United Feature Syndicate, Inc.
AND IT GOT ALL THE WAY UP INTO MY SINUSES
JIM DAVIS 12-6
IT WAS LIKE IT WAS FIZZING RIGHT INSIDE MY BRAIN!
YOU'VE JUST MADE HISTORY, JON
HEE, HEE, HEE
I CAN'T FINISH MY MEAL
GARFIELD

WHOOPS! THE OL' CLAW'S HOOKED A CARPET THREAD
UNNNGGGHHH!!!
...A LONG CARPET THREAD
JIM DAVIS 12-7
© 1987 United Feature Syndicate, Inc.
FOOD IS A DICHOTOMY
GARFIELD
FAT PEOPLE HATE TO LOVE IT
GARFIELD
JIM DAVIS 12-8
AND SKINNY PEOPLE LOVE TO HATE IT
GARFIELD
© 1987 United Feature Syndicate, Inc.

THERE'S NOTHING WORSE THAN BEING BORED
JIM DAVIS 12-9
HEY, THERE, MR. DROOPY FACE. LET ME ENTERTAIN YOU!
© 1987 United Feature Syndicate, Inc.
HOTCHA! HOTCHA!
I TAKE THAT BACK
CATS ARE POETRY IN MOTION
JIM DAVIS 12-10
© 1987 United Feature Syndicate, Inc.
TRIP
SPLAT
DOGS ARE GIBBERISH IN NEUTRAL

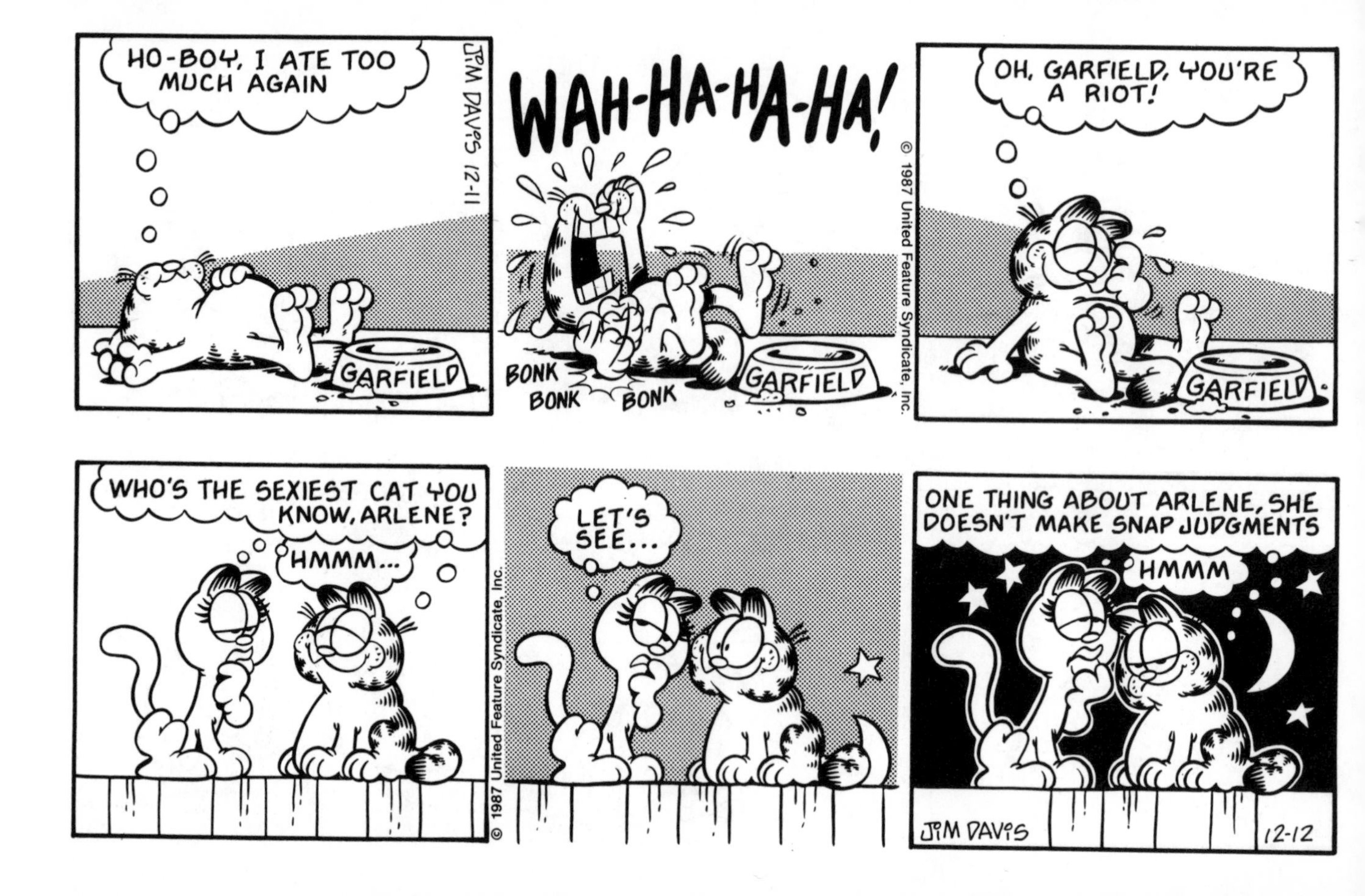
HO-BOY, I ATE TOO MUCH AGAIN
JIM DAVIS 12-11
WAH-HA-HA-HA!
BONK
BONK
BONK
GARFIELD
© 1987 United Feature Syndicate, Inc.
OH, GARFIELD, YOU'RE A RIOT!
GARFIELD
WHO'S THE SEXIEST CAT YOU KNOW, ARLENE?
HMMM...
© 1987 United Feature Syndicate, Inc.
LET'S SEE...
ONE THING ABOUT ARLENE, SHE DOESN'T MAKE SNAP JUDGMENTS
HMMM
JIM DAVIS
12-12

SLURP

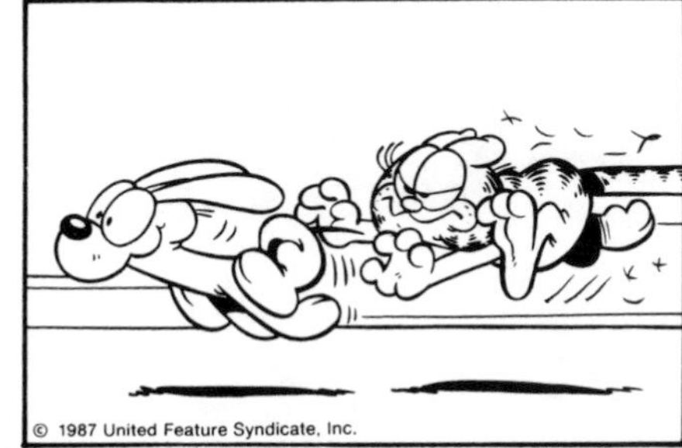
© 1987 United Feature Syndicate, Inc.

SCREEE

SLAM!
SCREEE

ODIE?

ODIE?
JIM DAVIS 12-13

SLURP

HERE'S A STORY ABOUT A CAT WHO TRAVELED 200 MILES TO FIND HIS OWNER
JIM DAVIS
© 1987 United Feature Syndicate, Inc.
CAN YOU IMAGINE YOU DOING THAT, GARFIELD?
HA! HA! HA!
I WOULD SEND A POSTCARD
12-14
IT SAYS HERE THAT MANY ARTISTS STARVE THEMSELVES IN THE SERVICE OF THEIR CRAFT
GARFIE
© 1987 United Feature Syndicate, Inc.
GLUCK
GARFIELD
A STARVING GLUTTON... I LIKE THAT
GARFIELD
JIM DAVIS 12-15

SIGH... A CAT'S WORK IS NEVER DONE
WHAT ARE YOU DOING, GARFIELD?
PLOP!
A CAT'S WORK
JIM DAVIS 12-16
© 1987 United Feature Syndicate, Inc.
SLAM!
IN CASE YOU'RE WONDERING WHERE I'VE BEEN AND WHAT I'VE BOUGHT, THAT'S NONE OF YOUR BUSINESS
I LOVE THE CHRISTMAS SEASON
JIM DAVIS 12-17
© 1987 United Feature Syndicate, Inc.

OUCH!
PSHHH
HEY, THIS ISN'T SHAVING CREAM!
AND THIS ISN'T TREE FLOCKING
JIM DAVIS 12-18
© 1987 United Feature Syndicate, Inc.
I SWEAR, GARFIELD
YOU GET MORE EXCITED ABOUT CHRISTMAS THAN ANY CHILD I KNOW!
I DO NOT!
JIM DAVIS 12-19
© 1987 United Feature Syndicate, Inc.

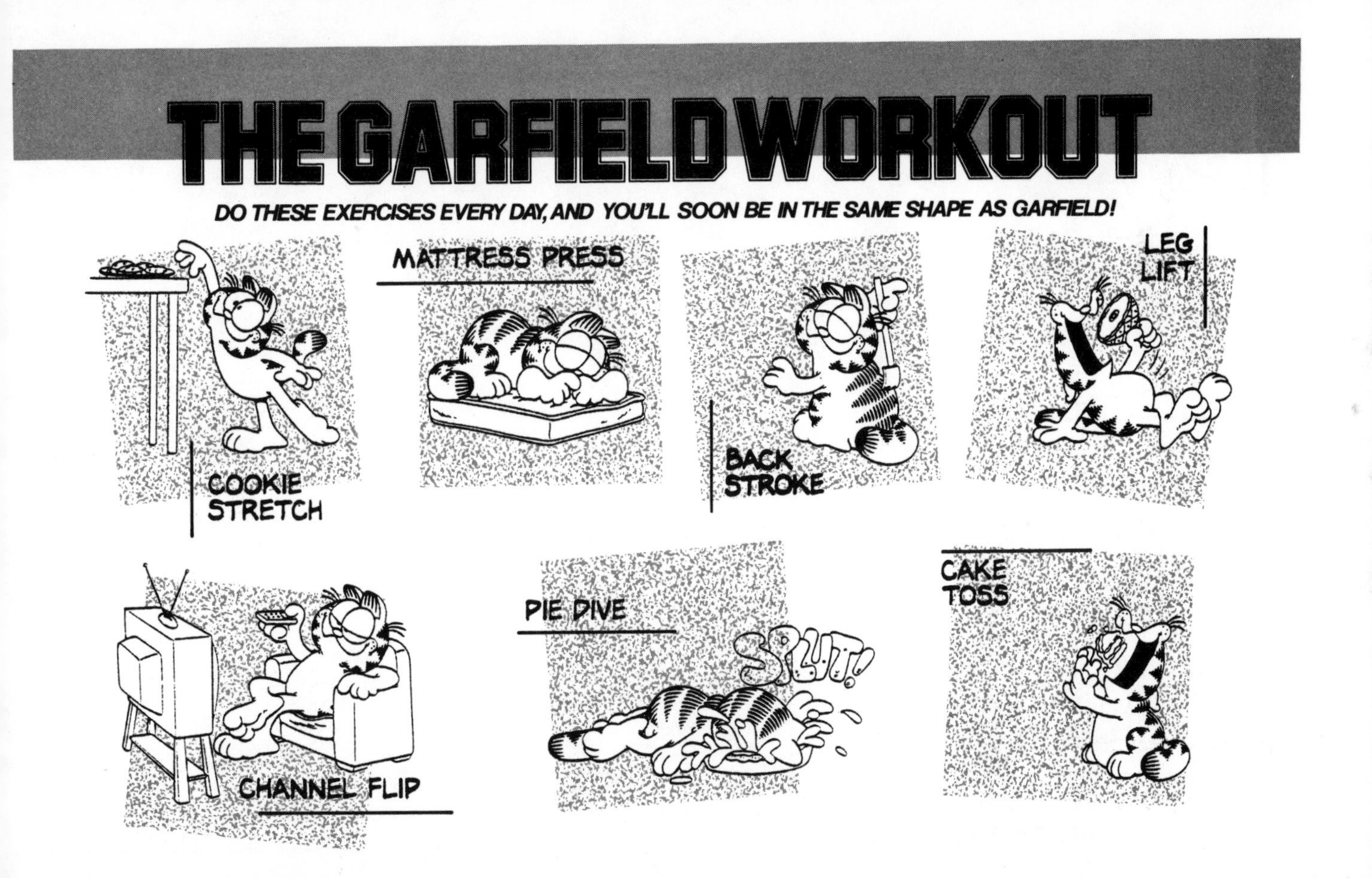

THE GARFIELD WORKOUT
DO THESE EXERCISES EVERY DAY, AND YOU'LL SOON BE IN THE SAME SHAPE AS GARFIELD!
COOKIE STRETCH
MATTRESS PRESS
BACK STROKE
LEG LIFT
CHANNEL FLIP
PIE DIVE
SPLUT!
CAKE TOSS